THE LUCK
OF POLITICS

THE LUCK
OF POLITICS

True tales of disaster and outrageous fortune

ANDREW LEIGH

Published by Black Inc.,
an imprint of Schwartz Publishing Pty Ltd
37–39 Langridge Street
Collingwood VIC 3066 Australia
enquiries@blackincbooks.com
www.blackincbooks.com

National Library of Australia Cataloguing-in-Publication entry:
Leigh, Andrew, 1972– author.
The luck of politics / Andrew Leigh.
9781863957557 (paperback)
9781925203394 (ebook)
Politicians – Australia – Anecdotes.
Australia – Politics and government – Anecdotes.
Australia – Politics and government – Miscellanea.
324.0994

Cover image: © goodze/iStock
Cover design by Peter Long
Text design by Tristan Main

Printed in Australia by Griffin Press. The paper this book is printed on is certified against the
Forest Stewardship Council® Standards. Griffin Press holds FSC chain of custody certification
SGS-COC-005088. FSC promotes environmentally responsible, socially beneficial and economically
viable management of the world's forests.

FSC
www.fsc.org
MIX
Paper from
responsible sources
FSC® C009448

CONTENTS

WHY POLITICS IS MORE LIKE POKER THAN CHESS

On the morning of 13 August 1940, a twin-propeller Lockheed Hudson took off from Melbourne to Canberra.[1] Among the ten passengers on board were three cabinet ministers in Robert Menzies' government: James Fairbairn, Henry Gullett and Geoffrey Street.

The trio covered vital wartime ministries: Fairbairn was responsible for civil aviation and the air, Gullett for scientific and industrial research, and Street for the army. All three were in Menzies' nine-member war cabinet. Also aboard the plane was the head of the army, Brudenell White, the man who masterminded the casualty-free evacuation of Gallipoli.

The ministers on board had twenty-eight years' parliamentary experience between them. But the lead pilot, Bob Hitchcock, was just twenty-eight years old. Hitchcock's flying record was spotty, and included a reprimand for a training incident in which his plane overturned on landing. After the incident, flight lieutenant Wilfred Compagnoni said of Hitchcock: 'After spending quite a few hours with him I realised that he would not make a pilot. It would have taken many hours and patience to make him even reasonably safe in an aeroplane.'[2] Another trainer recommended that he be removed from the course. But yet other officers saw Hitchcock as having promise, and he eventually passed his training and won promotion to flight lieutenant.

Today, if the air force was asked to provide a pilot for a plane carrying one-third of the cabinet, it would nominate a person with an exemplary record and decades of flying experience. But in 1940, Australia had been providing fifty pilots a year to the British air force. The ranks of experienced pilots were thin. So Bob Hitchcock – a man who had only a few years earlier flipped a plane while trying to land it – took the controls.

Luck has been a common theme in the Australian story. Indigenous Australians had elaborate rituals intended to bring good fortune to their community, and their traditional stories warned of locations that would bring bad luck. Luck mattered for white settlers too. In 1770, Captain James Cook's first voyage to Australia nearly ended in tragedy when his ship hit the Barrier Reef. The ship was only saved because a piece of coral lodged in a hole in the ship's hull. In the 1780s, Jean François de La Pérouse explored Australia, but died when his ship hit a coral reef in Micronesia. Had Cook been less fortunate and La Pérouse more so, French might be the official language of Australia today.[3] (Or Dutch, if the explorers of the 1600s had chanced to show more interest in establishing a colony on the west coast.)

Arthur Phillip's early convict settlement in Australia enjoyed its own good fortune. From climate historians, we know that the first years after the First Fleet's arrival were unseasonably cool and wet.[4] The colony did not experience drought until 1790, when it had been established for over two years and had built up freshwater supplies. Had Governor Phillip landed during the drought, the colony might not have survived.

In the nineteenth century, the colonies' greatest luck was the discovery of gold. So many immigrants poured in that Australia's population tripled in a decade. The lucky ones became rich, while the less fortunate eked out a living as best they could. By the end of the nineteenth century, average Australian living standards were the highest in the world.

As settlers explored the land, there were tales of luck and misfortune aplenty. Burke and Wills asked for their supply camp in Coopers Creek to be manned for four months. On their return, the explorers stopped for a day to bury a member of their party, and returned to Coopers Creek just nine hours after the supply team had departed.

Perhaps it's no surprise that some of Australia's favourite books – Albert Facey's *A Fortunate Life*, Donald Horne's *The Lucky Country*, and Paul Hasluck's *The Chance of Politics* – were focused on luck. Gambling, too, has been a recurring motif in Australian novels, including Frank Hardy's *Power Without Glory*, Jon Cleary's *The Sundowners* and Dymphna Cusack and Florence James's *Come in Spinner*.

In August 1940, the flight carrying three cabinet ministers made its way over Benalla, Hotham, Albury, Wagga and Cootamundra. There were scattered clouds along the way, but by the time it arrived in Canberra, the air had cleared. A light breeze was blowing from the north-west. As one newspaper report put it, 'Flying conditions were ideal'.[5]

In that era, the standard approach to landing a military plane was to bring it down to 300 metres, then complete a wide circuit of the airport, slowly descending. When the plane was down to about 150 metres, the pilot turned it into the wind, throttled back and lowered the flaps.

A bit before 11 am, watchers from the ground saw the Hudson approach Canberra airport and make a circuit. The wheels were lowered, and the flaps were down. Then, according to one report: 'It appeared as though the pilot had misjudged his height and decided not to land.' The plane rose and commenced a second circuit, longer and slower than the first. As it came towards a nearby hill, the left wing dropped suddenly, and the nose pointed towards the ground.

A plane stalls when air is passing over the wings too slowly for them to provide lift. The controls become sloppy, like a car in a skid. At high altitude, pilots are trained to recover from a stall by pointing the nose downwards, so the air starts to flow smoothly again over the wing. But when you're a few hundred metres from the ground, pointing the nose down isn't an option.

The Hudson slipped from side to side. On the ground, a ten-year-old boy was watching with his father. 'Dad, is he doing aerobatics?' the boy asked curiously. 'No,' the father replied, 'he's in trouble.' A second later, the plane corkscrewed twice and crashed into the ground. Immediately there was a dull explosion from one of the petrol tanks and a burst of flame. Black smoke billowed upwards. Everyone aboard died. A single crash had killed the head of the army and one-third of the cabinet.

♥

Luck has shaped the careers of some of the world's most famous politicians. In 1936, four generals led a coup to overthrow the Spanish government. Their leader, José Sanjurjo, prepared to fly back from exile in Portugal in a small plane. When the pilot queried the amount of baggage he was bringing, Sanjurjo replied, 'I need to wear proper clothes as the new *caudillo* of Spain.' The heavy luggage helped bring the plane down, killing Sanjurjo. In his place, General Franco became leader, ruling Spain for nearly forty years.

British prime minister Tony Blair lost the first time he stood as a candidate, and only won Labour preselection for a safe seat in 1983 following a last-minute redistribution and the decision of the assigned member to contest another electorate.[6] Eleven years later, Blair became leader of his party when the man expected to take Labour to victory in 1997, John Smith, had a heart attack while taking his morning bath.

Every election turns on a constellation of factors. It is unlikely that US president George H.W. Bush would have lost the 1992 election had Ross Perot not chosen to run, which split the right-wing vote. Conversely, his son George W. Bush only became president because Ralph Nader split the left-wing vote. Politicians have little control over those who choose to run against them.

And then there are the assassinations. Since the 1870s, there have been around 300 serious attempts to assassinate national leaders.[7] About one in five succeeded in killing their target. Whether an attacker hits or misses is largely a matter of chance, but the result can sometimes alter a nation's path. The 1963 murder of President John F. Kennedy, the 1984 shooting of Indian prime minister Indira Gandhi, and the 1986 killing of Swedish prime minister Olof Palme each had a deep impact on the national psyche of the respective nations.[8] The killers of presidential candidate Robert Kennedy and civil rights leader Martin Luther King in 1968 slowed the progress of race relations in the United States. It is true that political assassins aim to achieve a deliberate outcome, but they need luck for their terrible work to succeed.

For every unfortunate leader felled by an assassin, there are four who survive. When US president Theodore Roosevelt was shot in the chest in 1912, he was saved by the luck of having a folded fifty-page speech in his breast pocket.[9] In 1984, when an IRA bomb went off in the Grand Hotel in Brighton, British prime minister Margaret Thatcher happened not to be in the part of her suite where the blast hit. Seven years later, the IRA tried to kill her successor, John Major, by firing a shell containing 20 kilograms of Semtex at the prime minister's residence, 10 Downing Street. The shell landed in the garden about 30 metres from where the cabinet was meeting. Had it hit the room, the entire British cabinet would have been killed. Instead, history merely records Prime Minister Major saying to his colleagues: 'I think we'd better start again somewhere else.'[10]

Once a bullet enters your body, it's a matter of luck whether it hits vital organs or not. For Australian opposition leader Arthur Calwell, US president Ronald Reagan and Pope John Paul II, the fateful trajectory of a bullet meant that the attempts to assassinate them failed.

♠

Because there were no survivors, we'll never be sure what led to the 1940 air disaster. In his excellent book on the crash,

Cameron Hazlehurst notes that it could have been due to a mistake by Bob Hitchcock, the assigned pilot. Alternatively, it might have been caused by a mechanical error. It is even possible that Minister for Air James Fairbairn was at the controls and attempting to land the plane.[11]

What we can be sure about is that the 1940 crash changed the course of Australian politics. Menzies described it as 'the most devastating tragedy' in the history of government in Australia. Personally, Menzies was greatly affected by the loss of the three ministers and said he 'felt that for me the end of the world had come'.[12] Commentators regard the air crash as a major factor in Menzies losing the leadership of his party, and the conservatives losing office in 1941.

Yet there are others for whom the 1940 air disaster was the making of their careers. To the extent that the tragedy helped bring down a conservative government in 1941, it must equally have helped bring about the election of John Curtin's Labor government.

On the conservative side, one man whose career was changed forever by the air disaster was Harold Holt. In May 1940, Holt had taken leave from politics to serve as a gunner in the Second Australian Imperial Force. He had not resigned his seat, but expected to serve out the war in the army. After the crash, Menzies telephoned him. Would Holt return to the ministry? Holt said yes, and was soon elevated to cabinet. He remained active in the eight years his party was out of office, and then returned as a senior minister. By the time Menzies retired in 1966, Holt was his natural successor. We do not generally think of Holt as a lucky politician, but without the 1940 tragedy it is unlikely he would ever have become prime minister.

For others, the 1940 air disaster was a near miss. Prime Minister Robert Menzies' personal assistant booked him a seat on the doomed flight. When the assistant phoned Menzies to let him know of this, Menzies angrily told him to cancel – he preferred the train.[13] Similarly, Arthur Fadden (who served as prime minister briefly in 1941) was invited to join the flight, but already had a ticket on the train, so declined.[14] Had Menzies and Fadden enjoyed flying a little more, Australian political history would have followed a different path.

During the course of writing this book, I've often been asked why a sitting politician would write a book about luck. Why play down talent, effort and leadership in favour of fortune and misfortune?

It's certainly true that effort makes a difference in politics. If you're willing to wake before dawn, work weekends and sacrifice leisure time, you'll probably do better. Through practice, I've seen speakers change from mediocre to mellifluous. If you want to bring about positive change, there's little substitute for deep reading, talking and thinking. One theory of success is that you only get to the top after 10,000 hours of deliberate practice.[15] It's easy to imagine that this applies in politics too.

But while effort matters, it's a mistake to think that it's everything. While there are plenty of people who've gotten to the top by dint of hard work, many of those who've worked their guts out don't succeed. Effort may be a necessary condition for success, but it isn't a sufficient one. This means that for anyone watching politics, putting luck into the picture is like watching television in colour rather than black and white. Once you acknowledge the role of chance, you begin to notice how frequently luck shapes elections, careers and even laws.

Five hundred years ago, Niccolò Machiavelli argued that luck (which he called 'fortune') accounts for at least half of the outcomes in politics.[16] And yet the notion that luck matters a great deal in politics remains controversial. Part of the problem is that for too long politics has been told as a story of skilful winners and foolish losers. The best-selling political autobiographies are by successful leaders. It isn't surprising that their account is one that emphasises hard work and talent over good fortune.

But if history is written by the victors, and if winners underrate the role of chance, then we end up with an account of modern politics that shifts Lady Luck to the margins. Suppose everyone in the world puts on a blindfold and tries to solve a Rubik's Cube. One person succeeds. Unless we know that seven billion other people attempted the same feat, we might be tempted to assume that the winner did it through raw talent.

However, if it was only that luck puts colour into politics, I wouldn't have written this book. Understanding the role of chance doesn't just produce a more accurate perception of events – it also leads to a gentler view of success and failure. As an egalitarian, I've always been uncomfortable with the brutal notion of a world in which those who succeed are placed on a pedestal, while those who fail are kicked into the gutter.

In a series of experiments, psychologist Paul Piff brings subjects into the lab and randomly assigns them to be 'lucky' or 'unlucky'.[17] For example, participants are asked to play Monopoly with a twist: the lucky one gets $200 for passing go, and can roll two dice each turn. The unlucky one gets $100 for passing go, and can only roll one die. Pretty soon, Piff observes the lucky player taunting his opponent, banging the pieces and even eating more food from the snack bowl in the middle of the table. Lucky players begin behaving as though they are superior to their opponents.

Not every successful person is arrogant, but anyone who has spent time around sports stars, entertainers or multi-millionaires will know what Piff is getting at. Politics isn't immune from the temptation either. Treating the life stories of successful politicians as a roadmap can be a bit like reading a lottery winner's advice on how to get rich quick. Such accounts can end up giving a misleading perspective on success. As the baseball saying goes, 'Some people are born on third base, but go through life thinking they hit a triple'.[18]

Putting luck back into the picture reminds us that many of the outcomes in life are due to chances of birth, accidents of timing, and events entirely outside any one person's control. My belief in luck is a major reason why I support a targeted social safety net, which directs more resources towards the most disadvantaged. It's why I love living in a nation where audiences often don't stand up as the prime minister enters the room, where there aren't private areas on our beaches, and where most of us would prefer to be called 'mate', not 'sir' or 'madam'. Those who enjoy success aren't superior beings – they're fortunate souls, with an obligation to look after those who didn't receive the same opportunities. Because I'm an egalitarian, I believe in luck. And because I believe in luck, I regard excessive inequality as fundamentally unfair.[19]

Admittedly, there's a risk that someone writing about chance will start to see it everywhere, and misinterpret inevitable calamity and extraordinary skill as mere luck. Scientists call this 'confirmation bias', and I'll do my best to avoid it by combining stories with statistical analysis. Drawing on academic papers I co-authored as an economics professor and new data that I've crunched since then, I'll look at how genes affect electoral outcomes. Does it matter if candidates are male or female, beautiful or plain, Anglo or non-Anglo? Does the name your parents chose for you affect your political fortunes? How does the US economy affect Australian elections? And what about the weather on polling day? In each case, I'll study the numbers and separate fact from fantasy.

For too long, luck has been lurking in the political shadows; this book will bring it centre-stage. In so doing, not only will we gain a better understanding of events – but we will also see politics in a fresh light.

Many people think of politics as being like chess: a game of pure skill in which the better player always wins. There is no chance in chess, just an astoundingly large number of possible moves. A chess player's ability to out-think her opponent is all that determines who gets checkmated.

Poker is different. Chance determines whether players get dealt cards that are good or bad. Players try to work out what their opponents have, but they don't know for sure. Then they make a strategic decision, and more lucky (or unlucky) cards are dealt out. It helps to be a good poker player, but chance can be decisive. As past World Series of Poker champion Phil Hellmuth puts it, 'If there weren't luck involved, I would win every time.'

In chess, if your opponent moves their pawn to take your knight, there's no chance of a different outcome. Because chess is a game of pure skill, the best chess champions tend to win year after year. For example, India's Viswanathan Anand held the title of best chess player in the world from 2007 to 2013. But in Texas hold 'em poker, if you go all-in on pocket aces, you can expect to lose about a fifth of the time. Poker is a game of luck and skill. Over the past ten years, no-one has won the main event in the World Series of Poker more than once.

Politics is more like poker than chess. Skill matters, but even the most talented players can be dealt a bad hand, and even a rookie can get lucky. To discuss politics without taking into account the role of luck would be like commentating on a poker championship without once mentioning the dealer.

None of this implies that politicians cannot leave the world a better place. From Mahatma Gandhi to Aung San Suu Kyi, Thomas Jefferson to Nelson Mandela, individuals have shaped history for the better. My own decision to run for parliament was inspired by the principle that a life of service to others is a life well lived. I am acutely aware that progressive change requires rigorous solutions, forceful advocacy and deep engagement with the community. Striving to make a difference is not for the faint-hearted.

For all that, fortune can intervene. You might be as good at politics as Phil Hellmuth is at poker – but if you're dealt what card sharps call 'rags', then your best option is to fold. We need idealistic campaigners, kind altruists and inspiring leaders. But in a luck-strewn world, even the finest will sometimes flop. As Robert Kennedy summed up the problem: 'Only those who dare to fail greatly can ever achieve greatly.'

But what – exactly – do I mean by luck? Before diving into politics, let me make clear how I distinguish luck from skill, and how luck also helps shape success in fields as diverse as finance, sport, war and history.

2

WHAT IS LUCK?

This is a book about luck in politics. By 'luck', I mean *events that the individual concerned does not control or predict*. But just because it's out of *your* hands, it doesn't follow that the event is impossible to control or predict. Take coin tossing, for example. When you toss a coin in the air, the side that lands face up is determined by how hard you throw it, the wind conditions and what kind of surface it lands on. Whether the coin lands heads or tails is a matter of physics, not magic. But the point is that the person tossing the coin cannot control or predict the outcome.

Other games of chance have a similar character. The dealer's hand movements precisely determine how she shuffles a deck of cards. The strength with which the croupier spins the roulette wheel determines which pocket the ball falls into. If you ask Microsoft Excel to select a random number, it will use an algorithm based on your computer's internal clock at the moment you hit 'enter'.[1]

There's nothing mystical about these processes: they're just the interplay of physics and human decisions. In the nineteenth century, French mathematician Pierre-Simon Laplace argued that to an intellect that knew the positions of all atoms and directions of all forces, nothing would be unpredictable. The idea became known as 'Laplace's Demon'.[2]

The point is that the more ignorant you are about the world, the more things seem random. Before the nineteenth century, it was thought a person could not prevent catching a cold. Today, we recognise that washing your hands and avoiding close contact with sick people can reduce the risk. Better scientific knowledge makes a complicated world less unpredictable.

And yet science will never completely explain many of the outcomes in politics. Would-be politicians must roll the dice: many things in life are outside their control. The accident of birth, the luck of who your opponents turn out to be, the fortune of weather and the unpredictability of global circumstances are all factors that shape political careers and policy outcomes.

Luck was a familiar concept to the ancient Greeks and ancient Romans, for whom the goddesses Tyche and Fortuna, respectively, were the forerunners to today's 'Lady Luck'. Indeed, the ancient Athenians chose most office-holders by lot, in a system known as 'sortition'.[3] Among eligible citizens, random selection determined who sat on the governing council, as well as who served as roadway officials, temple guardians, tax collectors, superintendents of feasts, judges, sacrificers and so on. The ruler of Athens was also chosen by lottery. Because that person only held office for one day, at least a quarter of Athenian citizens ruled their city-state at some stage.[4] So seriously did the Athenians take random selection that they invented a special machine, the kleroterion, to carry out the lottery. In effect, Athens' stone Powerball machine decided who would be ruler for the day.

But while some ancient cultures institutionalised the role of luck, the past two thousand years have seen the notion of chance pushed to the margins. Most religions take the view that life outcomes are determined by destiny, not fortune. The Bible states that 'The lot is cast into the lap, but its every decision is from the Lord'. Similarly, Islam teaches that Allah is all-knowing, all-seeing and all-powerful. According to the Koran, humans have the freedom to choose only within constraints imposed by Allah. And in Buddhism, the notion of karma denies the idea of luck. In Buddha's words: 'Fools wait for a lucky day, but every day is a lucky day for an industrious man.'

It was not until the 1400s that the word 'luck' entered the English language, as a derivation of the old German word *gelücke*.[5] As dice and card games became more common, the word spread. By the 1600s, it was not just soldiers who were playing games of chance, but royalty too, with diarist Samuel Pepys describing the gambling mania that swept the court of Charles II. In that century, several mathematicians formalised the idea of probability, including Pierre de Fermat, Christiaan Huygens and Blaise Pascal. As Nicholas Rescher puts it, 'In the order of historical causes and effects, the mathematical calculus of probability can be traced to the gambling mania of the soldiers of the Thirty Years' War.'[6]

In a classic essay, American philosopher Thomas Nagel identified three different types of luck.[7] The first is constitutive luck, which is the luck of your genes or upbringing. There is luck in being born male or female, short or tall, quick-witted or slow. And perhaps, Nagel suggests, there may be some element of luck in personality – how generous or selfish a person is, whether they tend to be extroverted or introverted.

The second is circumstantial luck, meaning the surroundings in which you find yourself. Nagel gives the example of someone holding fascist beliefs. Should they happen to be an adult in 1930s Germany, they might commit atrocities, yet in another time or place they might do no harm to anyone.

The third type of luck is resultant luck, which is the way things turn out, based on your actions. Nagel gives the example of a driver who runs a red light and inadvertently kills a child. His action is no different than if the intersection had been empty, but his resultant luck means that the consequences are quite different. In this book, you will see examples of these three types of luck – constitutive luck, circumstantial luck and resultant luck – as they affect outcomes in politics.

When you start to look carefully at society, luck is everywhere. In my previous book, *The Economics of Just About Everything*, I listed some of the ways that luck affects Australian sport. Because youth sports inadvertently favour children who are the oldest in the team, elite sportspeople are more likely to be born just after the age cut-off. There are twice as many NRL players born in January as December, and twice as many Matildas and Socceroos born in August as July. In soccer, a player whose shot on goal hits the post is rated more talented if the ball bounces in than if it bounces out. In cricket, it helps to debut on a familiar pitch, so a batsman who debuts at home rather than abroad ends up with a career average one-fifth higher. The cricket team that wins the toss in a day–night match raises its odds of victory by 4 percentage points.

In elite sport, genetic luck matters more than ever.[8] Over the past generation, the share of NBA basketball players who are more than 7 feet tall has doubled, to one in ten. Meanwhile, the average height of elite female gymnasts has shrunk from 5'3" to 4'9". Swimmers are increasingly likely to have long torsos and stumpy legs. The arm span of basketballers tends to exceed their height. Fewer than one in 1000 people in the world are Kalenjin Kenyans, but their slender limbs and high red-blood-cell count means they dominate international marathons. If you haven't got the lucky genes for your favourite sport, your chances of making the Olympics have never been worse.

In the financial markets, too, luck matters. On 16 January 1995, Nick Leeson, a trader at merchant bank Barings, placed a 'short straddle' in the Singapore and Tokyo stock exchanges.[9] In effect, Leeson was betting that the markets would not move significantly overnight. Then the Kobe earthquake hit, and the loss ballooned to over a billion dollars. Barings Bank, which had operated for more than 230 years, collapsed the next month.

In the field of science, many inventions have an element of serendipity about them.[10] The original work on penicillin began when Alexander Fleming left open a petri dish, which grew blue-green mould. Louis Pasteur's cholera vaccine was developed after a batch of bacteria was accidentally allowed to sit around for a few weeks. The artificial sweetener saccharin was discovered when a researcher working on coal tar forgot to wash his hands before eating dinner. Viagra was originally trialled as a way of treating heart disease. It failed at its intended purpose, but scientists noticed that it had a surprising side-effect on men. Luck also played a role in the discovery of snow-making, Teflon, nylon, stainless steel, the microwave oven and cling wrap.

Medical research can be lucky in other ways. In the 1970s, the United States' War on Cancer saw millions of dollars poured into understanding the role that retroviruses play in causing cancer. The research effort did little to reduce cancer death rates, but that retrovirus research proved vital when HIV/AIDS was discovered in the 1980s. Without the War on Cancer, thousands more people would have died of AIDS.[11]

Luck also affects the timing of discovery. Historians of science have noted the frequency with which two independent researchers arrive at a discovery at almost the same moment.[12] Four independent scientists discovered sunspots around 1611. Isaac Newton and Gottfried Leibniz independently discovered calculus in the 1680s (with Leibniz starting first with integration and Newton with differentiation). In 1847, four scientists independently derived the law of conservation of energy. Charles Darwin and Alfred Wallace separately developed the theory of evolution in the 1850s. On the same day, Valentine's Day 1876, Elisha Gray and Alexander Graham Bell both filed a patent for invention of the telephone. There are two independent discoverers of oxygen, two inventors of colour photography, three inventors of decimals, and three inventors of logarithms. Five people claimed to have invented the steamboat, six said they invented the thermometer, and nine claimed to have invented the telescope. In all these cases, it is surely a matter of luck who receives the fame and fortune as the 'true inventor' of a breakthrough.

On the battlefield, it may be politicians who choose whether to send troops to war, but the results of conflict are often shaped by luck. As Napoleon Bonaparte liked to say, 'I would rather have a general who is lucky than one who is good'. Napoleon would have been well aware of the events of 1588, when Spain's King Phillip II sent 130 ships to invade England. A freak storm in the English Channel hit the ships, destroying one-third of the 'Invincible Armada', and perhaps changing the outcome of the battle.[13]

On 28 June 1914, six amateur assassins waited by a major road in Sarajevo for Austrian archduke Franz Ferdinand. But when the motorcade reached them, most lost their nerve. One man threw a bomb, which bounced off the archduke's car. Seeing that the attempt had failed, the other assassins slipped into the crowd. Some time later, thinking that the archduke was out of danger, the motorcade took a wrong turn onto a narrow street. Waiting for them was a member of the assassination team, Gavrilo Princip. He stepped up and fired two shots. The death of the archduke provided the pretext Austria needed for war with Serbia. World War I followed.[14]

In 1931, Englishman John Scott-Ellis was taking his red Fiat for a drive around Munich when a pedestrian stepped off the kerb without looking. The car knocked him down, but he regained his feet. As Ed Smith recounts the tale, the driver and pedestrian met a few years later – leaving Scott-Ellis in no doubt as to the identity of the man he had injured.[15] In subsequent decades, Scott-Ellis often told the story of the accident, and wondered aloud how history might have been different if his car had been going faster when it struck Adolf Hitler. (A similar but slightly less credible story suggests that in the final weeks of World War I, British soldier Henry Tandey had the chance to shoot Hitler, but chose not to because the German was wounded and retreating.[16])

At the end of World War II, the Americans set out to drop

a second nuclear bomb on Japan. The weapon, 'Fat Man', was originally destined for Kokura,[17] but on the day there was heavy cloud and smoke over that city. So the B-29 bomber flew south and dropped the bomb on its secondary target, Nagasaki. Most of the 40,000 to 80,000 people who died were civilians. Because Nagasaki was a bigger city than Kokura, it is likely that the cloud cover over the original target increased the death toll by around 10,000 people.[18]

The Cold War created its own share of near misses.[19] In 1960, computers at the North American Air Defense Command and Colorado Springs predicted, with what they said was 99.9% certainty, that the Soviet Union had launched an all-out missile attack. The system turned out to have misinterpreted an image of the moon rising. In 1979, the computer again warned of a full-scale attack. After missiles were placed on alert and bombers manned, it turned out that someone had mistakenly put a war-game tape into the computer. In 1980, the same systems warned that 220 missiles were headed towards the United States. The error was caused by a defective computer chip worth less than a dollar. In 1995, Boris Yeltsin had less than six minutes to decide whether to respond to Russian reports of a missile heading towards Moscow. It turned out to be a Norwegian weather rocket.

On an individual basis, luck affected soldiers everywhere. As Erich Remarque wrote in *All Quiet on the Western Front*, 'It is just as much a matter of chance that I am still alive as that I might have been hit. In a bomb-proof dug-out I may be smashed to atoms and in the open may survive ten hours' bombardment unscratched. No soldier outlives a thousand chances. But every soldier believes in Chance and trusts his luck.'[20]

War historian Brad Manera told me the story of a West Australian soldier who felt a blow to the face when he landed with the 11th Battalion on the shores of Gallipoli in April 1915.[21] When he returned from the war, the soldier ran a pub in Fremantle, but suffered particularly bad mood swings and a foul temper. One day the man fell down the stairs and landed on his face. Out of his nose popped a Turkish rifle bullet, which had ricocheted off the Gallipoli shale and lodged at the front of his brain. Bullet gone, the man became as kind-natured as he had been in his youth.

More recently, Ryan Mathison, a lance corporal, was on patrol in Afghanistan when he stepped on a bomb containing 10 kilograms of explosives. The detonation cap exploded, but the bomb did not. As the journalist who recounted Mathison's story observed, 'If luck is the battlefield's final arbiter – the wild card that can trump fitness, training, teamwork, equipment, character and skill – then Lance Corporal Ryan T. Mathison experienced its purest and most welcome form.'[22]

It isn't only combatants who are affected by the luck of war. In 1940, the British government, in what Churchill would later describe as 'a deplorable and regrettable mistake', expelled over two thousand men and boys, most of whom were Jewish refugees from Germany and Austria. Two days after departing Liverpool, their ship – the *Dunera* – was fired upon by a German U-boat. The torpedoes failed to explode. Indeed, one account suggests that a torpedo might have hit the ship, but malfunctioned.[23]

The ship eventually reached Australia, and the passengers, who came to be known as 'the *Dunera* boys',[24] included a disproportionate number of our future intellectual leaders. Kurt

Baier was a professor of philosophy at the Australian National University. Hans Buchdahl was a leading professor of theoretical physics at the same institution. Henry Mayer was a leading political scientist at the University of Sydney. Hugo Wolfsohn ran the political science department at La Trobe University.

Among economists, the most famous *Dunera* boy is Fred Gruen, the head of economics in the Australian National University's Research School of Social Sciences. Fred Gruen was among Gough Whitlam's key economic policy advisers, and Fred's two sons – David and Nicholas – are today among our most influential public policy economists. Without a torpedo malfunction, Australia's post-war intellectual history would have been considerably weaker.[25]

Luck can shape the course of nations. Like the chance that accompanied Cook's sea voyage to Australia, random factors determined when many countries were colonised by European powers. Until the longitude problem was solved, exploration in the Pacific was basically a matter of sailing around the southern tip of South America, travelling up the Chilean coast and heading west on a constant latitude. This meant that islands were more likely to be discovered by explorers if they were in areas with good east–west winds and favourable currents. Hence Guam was colonised in the 1500s, while Micronesian states such as Fefan and Pohnpei were not colonised until nearly two centuries later.[26]

Other researchers have shown that colonialism was strongly affected by the risks posed to settlers by diseases such as malaria and yellow fever.[27] In Nigeria, Gambia and Sierra Leone, the death rate for early European settlers was over 50% a year. As a result, colonial powers were much more reluctant to establish significant settlements. Indeed, the British government originally considered establishing convict settlements in West Africa, but opted for Australia because the death rate in Africa was considered too high even for convicts.

Going back still further, economic historian Justin Cook contends that the genetic quirk which enables certain peoples to tolerate milk into adulthood was a powerful advantage for economic development.[28] It meant that northern Europeans (who tend to produce the lactase enzyme as adults) could enjoy a better diet than those in Sub-Saharan Africa (who are less likely to do so). This meant higher living standards, better technologies and bigger armies.

In a similar vein, geographer Jared Diamond asks why Europeans colonised Africa and the Americas, rather than the other way around. He concludes that Europe benefited from two lucky advantages: plants and animals that were suitable for domestication, and a wide east–west span, which allowed populations to spread while remaining in similar climatic conditions.[29]

Diamond also highlights the way that small differences in initial conditions can have massive effects. At first glance, Britain and Japan look like mirror images: small islands adjacent to a well-populated landmass. Yet while Britain was invaded five times between AD 43 and 1688, there was no successful attempt to invade Japan in the same period. The difference, Diamond argues, is that while the sea journey from France to Britain is 35 kilometres, the distance from Korea to Japan is 180 kilometres.[30]

Recalling Laplace's Demon, it's true that shifts of tectonic plates are driven by the laws of physics, but to the average person in Britain or Japan, such effects are as random as a dice roll. Yet variations in undersea geology made the difference between repeated invasions and autonomy, shaping the lives of millions of people.

For the past two centuries, Australia has had the good fortune to develop into one of the world's most robust democracies, with one of the highest standards of living. Yet there were at least four moments when Australian history could easily have taken a different path.

In the 1850s, the colonial authorities initially chose to prescribe an extremely small claim size for goldminers: eight feet by eight feet.[31] Historians differ on whether this was good luck or good management, but its effect was to spread the 'lottery' of goldmining across a large group of self-employed miners, who then helped spur the transition to democracy.[32] The alternative would have been much larger claim sizes, with mining carried out by wage labour (the contrast to Australia's experience is Sierra Leone, where an elite monopoly over diamond mining set the stage for authoritarian rule after independence).[33]

Another tipping point, also in the mid-1800s, was the attempt by pastoral leaseholders ('squatters'), to convert their leases into freehold title. Instead, colonial governments chose to reallocate millions of hectares to ordinary farmers ('selectors'). The result was a much more equal distribution of land. If the squatters had won, they would likely have entrenched a 'squattocracy', similar to the enormous landholdings that persisted in Argentina through to the twentieth century. Economic historian Ian McLean argues that it was only pressure from Britain that tipped the balance in favour of the selectors over the squatters, and led to a more egalitarian and democratic Australia.[34]

A third moment at which Australia's economic trajectory could have taken a different path was the 1880s, when an attempt to establish a separate colony in northern Queensland was vetoed by the British colonial authorities. Some suggest that such a colony might have consisted of an aristocracy of white planters relying on indentured labour from the nearby Pacific Islands. This kind of experiment would have looked more like the Caribbean, or the antebellum south of the United States, and might well have produced similarly poor long-run growth outcomes. As Geoffrey Blainey describes Britain's decision to veto the new colony: 'At the time it seemed a decision of no great importance but it probably prevented the emergence of a seventh colony which could have become a stronghold of coloured labour.'[35]

Finally, there was the unexpected increase in commodity prices that occurred in the first decade of the twenty-first century. In that period, the iron ore price rose tenfold, and average commodity prices tripled. With Australia the world's biggest producer of iron ore, the effect was to massively boost our economy. By the end of the decade, the mining and mining-related sectors, which together account for around one-fifth of the economy, contributed more than two-thirds of all economic growth.[36] China's rise was Australia's luck.

In parliament, the conversation about luck has waxed and waned since Federation. In Figure 1, I plot the frequency of mentions of the words 'luck', 'chance' and 'fate' in parliamentary debates.[37] Mentions were plentiful in the 1920s, 1950s and late-1990s. Conversely, politicians were less likely to talk about luck in times of crisis, such as the 1930s Depression, the world wars, and the 1970s oil shocks. Politicians were twice as likely to talk about luck in 1945, the year World War II ended, than in the early 1940s, when we were in the depths of the war. The peak years for the luck conversation in parliament – 1921, 1924, 1954 and 1969 – were all comfortable years for Australia as a nation. Reading through some of the speeches that mention luck, it struck me that parliamentarians seem more inclined to refer to good luck than bad luck.

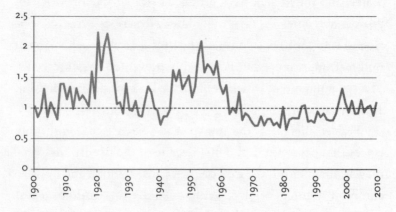

Figure 1: When do politicians talk about luck?

♦

In this chapter, I have outlined how luck has shaped our democracy and our economy, affecting scientists, sailors and soldiers alike. All of us are affected by luck. And yet professions differ markedly in how readily they accept the role of chance.

In sport, superstitions are extremely common. As Matthew Syed and Ed Smith have noted, some sportspeople develop ridiculous habits in an attempt to keep the luck flowing.[38] Baseball player Jim Ohms put a coin in his jockstrap after every winning match. Rugby's David Campese insisted on sitting next to the bus driver for every away match. Soccer player Kolo Touré has to be the last player to leave the dressing room. Tennis player Venus Williams has to tie her shoelaces a certain way and bounce the ball precisely five times before serving.

By contrast, politicians are rarely superstitious, and there are ready alternative explanations for their superstitious tics, should they have any. Yes, some of my colleagues wear 'lucky ties' when they're giving a big speech (like Jed Bartlett on *The West Wing*). But it's also reasonable to want to look your best at important moments. True, Barack Obama always plays basketball on election day.[39] But as a man who enjoys the sport, he may simply see it as a way to relax. The current Liberal Party director always visits the Sydney Town Hall on election day – but it happens that he learns a lot from one of the nation's biggest polling booths.[40]

For most politicians, the journey to parliament begins with being selected by a party. The luck of winning preselection is one of the most under-recognised aspects of politics, so let's turn now to the question of how parties choose their candidates.

3

POLITICAL PARENTS, SLIDING DOORS AND THE DAUGHTER EFFECT – THE LUCK OF PRESELECTION

On Saturday, 14 July 2007, Michael Towke won preselection for the safe Liberal seat of Cook, in Sydney's south. The balloting saw his rivals successively eliminated – beginning with Scott Morrison, who garnered just 8 votes. Towke also beat Paul Fletcher (now the member for Bradfield) and David Coleman (now the member for Banks). In the fourth and final round, Towke won with 82 votes to 70.

The week after the preselection, questions began to surface about Towke's credentials. How many years had he been a member of the Labor Party? Why had the security firm he ran not filed recent annual returns? The Liberal Party state executive could not reach a consensus on what should be done, so the decision went to a ballot and Towke's preselection was overturned by a vote of 11 to 9. A new preselection panel was formed, and on 23 August, Scott Morrison defeated businessman Peter Tynan by 26 votes to 14.

Morrison is now a senior cabinet minister, but it's easy to see how luck could have seen that position go to someone else.

If Coleman, Fletcher or Tynan had won the first preselection, the state executive would not have overturned it. If the Sydney media had not dug into Towke's background, the state executive would not have raised concerns. If two of the eleven state executive members who supported overturning the ballot had changed their minds, Towke would have remained the Liberal candidate. And if the conservative bloc who backed Towke in the first preselection had opted for Tynan over Morrison in the second ballot, Tynan would have won.

One way in which luck affects preselections is that the calibre of the other candidates is outside your control. It's like standing on a busy street trying to get a taxi. Yes, you have to have an outstretched arm and some money in your wallet. But that doesn't help if there's another person up the road who hails the taxi first.

Because so much in politics is interconnected, the bad luck of Coleman and Fletcher in the 2007 Cook preselection also translated into someone else's bad luck in the seats where they were ultimately chosen. Two years later, Fletcher defeated Julian Leeser by 60 votes to 51 in the Bradfield preselection (Coleman was a candidate in that race, as was John Alexander, now member for Bennelong). In 2012, Coleman defeated Ron Delezio by 60 to 33 to win Liberal preselection for the seat of Banks. The cascade of events in the Cook preselection ultimately affected Leeser and Delezio – perhaps one of whom would be in parliament today if things had gone differently in Cook.

For some people, missing out in one race opens opportunities in others. Gough Whitlam won preselection for the state seat of Sutherland in 1950, and missed out on being elected by just 456 votes. Similarly, John Howard missed out on being elected to the state seat of Drummoyne in 1968 by 420 votes. In both cases, just one-fiftieth of voters would have had to switch in order to send a future prime minister into state parliament.

Howard reflects: 'I think back how fortunate I was to have lost; and no doubt [Whitlam] did [too]. If I had won that seat, I might have been in state parliament for a term or two and then would have lost and then people would have said, well, he was a lousy local member, that's why he lost. And they would have said the same about Whitlam, that he hadn't connected with his people.'[1] In each case, their failure to win a marginal state seat left Whitlam and Howard able to contest a preselection for a safe federal seat. Indeed, Whitlam was also unsuccessful at entering local government. With classic immodesty, he reflected: 'I might have been Lord Mayor of Sydney, or Premier of New South Wales or even President of the Sutherland Shire. Alas, the fates were against me.'[2]

In 1989, Mark Latham was declared the winner – by two votes – in a preselection for the state seat of Liverpool. After a protest, the ALP National Executive overturned the ballot and installed another candidate.[3] Had Latham won the Liverpool preselection, he might not have been able to move into federal politics when a preselection opened up for the federal seat of Werriwa just four years later. Latham's loss in a state preselection probably helped his chances of getting federal preselection.

In my own case, running for preselection always depended on gaining the support of my wife, Gweneth. When my predecessor, Bob McMullan, announced his resignation, Gweneth and I had just celebrated our sixth wedding anniversary with a dinner at which we complimented ourselves on getting the work–life balance just right. In the first few days after McMullan's resignation became public, I gained the impression that Gweneth had vetoed my running for preselection, and resigned myself to staying in academia. But then she said yes.

There were eight candidates in the preselection for Fraser, among them a community organiser, a disability rights activist, an Indigenous businessman and a senior official of the ALP.[4] If Gweneth had said 'no' to my candidacy, the preselection would have been won by George Williams, one of Australia's leading constitutional law experts. (He wasn't the eventual runner-up, but trust me when I tell you that's the way the result would have gone.) George and I are of similar ages, and were both university professors with young families, so it's no surprise that we had a similar support base. In a parallel universe, George would be a terrific member for Fraser.

There was plenty of luck in my preselection. One aspect was timing: I would not have won if Bob McMullan's resignation had been anticipated (since other candidates would likely have been able to enlist more supporters), nor if the preselection had been held within weeks of Bob's resignation. The only reason I was able to win the Fraser preselection is because it was a three-month campaign in which many of the 241 preselectors were undecided at the outset.

After a victory, we may look back on an individual's career and decide its course was inevitable. But things are often more finely balanced. Julia Gillard missed out on Labor preselection for the seat of Melbourne in 1993. In 1996, she was the third candidate on Labor's Senate ticket in Victoria. Labor had won three Senate spots in the previous election, and would do so again in the next election. But in 1996, after six weeks of counting, it was announced that Gillard had missed out. It was not until 1998 that Gillard won preselection for the seat of Lalor. Julia Gillard only got into federal parliament on her third attempt. Moreover, if her second attempt had succeeded, Senator Gillard would likely have had quite a different political career. She would probably have become a senior cabinet minister, but could not have become deputy prime minister or prime minister, positions restricted to members of the House of Representatives.

In Paul Keating's 1968 preselection for Blaxland, the count at the end of the day had him with 108 votes, trailing left candidate Bill Junor, who had 124 votes. Forty-nine ballots had been challenged and were yet to be counted. At issue was the eligibility of people in certain branches to vote. The Credentials Committee had earlier ruled on the matter, but after this new challenge, the votes were reassessed. Party officials eventually declared 39 of them to be valid, of which 38 went to Keating. Keating won by 146 votes to Junor's 125 votes.[5]

In a fluid contest like a preselection, Keating's 54% victory counts as exceptionally close. But it's far from unique. Peter Baldwin won his first preselection with 53% of the vote, Malcolm Turnbull with 56%, Brian Howe with 56% and Gough Whitlam with 59%.[6] Moreover, many of those who narrowly missed out in a close preselection failed to subsequently win preselection for a different seat. Sliding doors often stay shut.

Even after being preselected, luck matters. During the 1996 election campaign, Liberal Party candidate Pauline Hanson argued for the abolition of government programs that provided assistance to Indigenous Australians. As a result, she was disendorsed by the Liberal Party. However, because the ballot papers had already been printed, voters in the seat of Oxley saw the words 'Liberal Party' beneath her name, and many would have voted for her thinking that she was the authorised Liberal Party candidate. Had Hanson made her comments a little earlier in the election campaign, the Liberal Party would have run a candidate against her, and she most likely would not have won Oxley. The luck of timing helped bring Hanson into parliament.

To look at just how competitive the preselection process is, I analysed the results of a confidential survey of federal political candidates carried out by the Australian National University. I found that in preselections for major parties, there was an average of six candidates.[7] And beyond these candidates, there were surely many more who weighed the odds and opted not to enter the race.

One of the factors that affects whether a candidate wins preselection is their gender. One of the reasons that women are underrepresented in parliament is that (at least in the data I analysed), their odds of winning preselection were lower than those of men. This particularly holds true in the Coalition parties. Consequently, one-third of Labor candidates in the 2013 election were women, but just one-fifth of Coalition candidates.[8]

Why does the Coalition field fewer women candidates? One possibility is that women candidates tend to be more left-wing than male candidates. For example, relative to men in the same party, female candidates tend to be less worried about union power, but more worried about the power of big business.[9] On taxation, education and defence, women candidates hold more left-wing views than male candidates from the same party. If preselectors tend to prefer candidates who are more ideologically extreme, then it will follow that women would be more appealing to Labor preselectors, but less appealing to Coalition preselectors.

Yet this is only part of the answer. A significant factor in the Labor Party is the party's 1994 decision to enact an affirmative action policy.[10] This rule required that in the first election following the year 2001, women had to comprise at least 35% of Labor candidates in winnable seats. Passed at a time when there was only one woman in cabinet, the reform boosted the number of women standing for winnable Labor seats. The 1996 and 1998 elections saw Julia Gillard, Jenny Macklin, Tanya Plibersek and Nicola Roxon enter parliament for the Labor Party. All four would end up in cabinet. They are indisputably talented and hard-working politicians, but they were also fortunate to be seeking preselection at a time when Labor had reformed its rules. Had women as impressive as Gillard, Macklin, Plibersek and Roxon sought Labor preselection in the late 1970s, it is hard to imagine that they would have been as successful.

Noting the impact of gender in preselection takes nothing away from the calibre of candidates. My own preselection for Fraser (the north part of the ACT) was held at the same time as preselection for the other House of Representatives electorate of Canberra (the south of the ACT). Northsiders were looking for a replacement for Bob McMullan, while southsiders were seeking a replacement for Annette Ellis. I doubt it's a coincidence that southsiders chose Gai Brodtmann, a woman with deep community experience like Annette, while northsiders chose one glasses-wearing man to replace another. If the

Australian National University had been located southside, it's likely I would have chosen to live there – which means I would now be an academic rather than a parliamentarian. Such is the luck of preselection.

Just as gender is a form of luck, so too are our parents' occupations. In politics, much has been made of the role of dynasties: families in which children follow their parents into parliament. Since 1901, nearly 1650 people have served as members or senators. Of these, thirty followed their mother or (more commonly) father into federal parliament. So the share of 'dynastic' parliamentarians is a bit under 2%.

Should we regard 2% as a large or small number? On the one hand, it implies that 98% of parliamentarians have no direct political pedigree. On the other hand, children of federal politicians are clearly massively overrepresented compared to the general population. Since Federation, nearly thirty million Australians have been eligible to stand for parliament, so the share of people who have ever served in the national parliament is just 0.006%.[11] Put another way, children of federal parliamentarians are over 300 times more likely to serve in parliament than children of non-parliamentarians.

To gauge the dynastic bias, Table 1 compares the occupation of parliamentarians with nine other occupations: primary school teachers, lawyers, electricians, truck drivers, accountants, police officers, miners, GPs and ministers of religion. For each of these occupations, there is evidence of some dynastic bias.[12] For example, lawyers' children are four times more likely to become lawyers than children of non-lawyers, while police officers' children are twelve times more likely to become police officers. However, the degree of overrepresentation ranges between about three and sixty: well below the level of dynastic bias in federal politics.[13] Even so, the level of dynastic bias in Australian politics is below what has been estimated for the United States (probably by a large margin, since the dynastic bias in the US sample is likely an underestimate).[14]

Table 1: Dynastic bias among parliamentarians and other occupations

	PERCENTAGE WITH PARENT IN SAME OCCUPATION	PERCENTAGE OF PARENTS IN AUSTRALIA IN EACH OCCUPATION	DYNASTIC BIAS
Primary school teachers	6.7	2.0	3.3
Lawyers	1.2	0.3	4.0
Electricians	5.5	1.0	5.5
Truck drivers	10.6	1.9	5.7
Accountants	8.1	1.3	6.4
Police officers	5.1	0.4	12.0
Miners	12.0	0.5	22.9
GPs	16.1	0.4	37.9
Ministers of religion	17.8	0.3	61.2
Federal parliamentarians (Australia)	1.8	0.006	324.3
Federal parliamentarians (United States)	3.6	0.1	354.1

Having a politician as a parent certainly raises the chances that a child will enter parliament. But there is little evidence that these children underperform their parents, at least on the most readily observable measures. If political dynasties were pure nepotism, then we might expect that children of politicians –

like movie sequels – would do worse than the original. However, compared with their parents, children of politicians serve in parliament for a year longer, and serve in the ministry for one-and-a-half years longer. There is no doubt that the luck of having a political parent helps a candidate win preselection, but those candidates do not appear to crash and burn any more frequently than did their parents.

Even if a parliamentarian's children don't run for office, they can have a strong impact. Famously, when his daughter Rosslyn's heroin addiction reached crisis point in 1984, Prime Minister Bob Hawke came 'within minutes of resigning from office'.[15] Prime Minister John Howard's traditional attitudes about child rearing evolved as his daughter Melanie grew up. Howard's introduction of the 30% child-care rebate coincided with the point when his daughter Melanie was a successful lawyer and looking to have children.[16] Victorian Premier Denis Napthine choked back tears as he signed the state up to the National Disability Insurance Scheme, thinking of his severely autistic foster son.[17] Addressing the 2014 International Women's Day breakfast in Parliament House, Prime Minister Tony Abbott described how his own attitudes had evolved: 'What is it that turns an unreconstructed bloke into a feminist? Three daughters.'[18]

Might the gender of parliamentarians' children affect the party they choose? To test this, I compiled data on the children of MPs and senators in the forty-fourth parliament. Table 2 shows the results.[19] On average, parliamentarians have a similar number of sons (0.8) as daughters (0.9), but the gap is larger for certain groups. Male Labor parliamentarians have about 50% more daughters than sons, while female Coalition parliamentarians have about 50% more sons than daughters.[20]

What's special about Labor men and Coalition women? As we have seen, female politicians tend to be more left-wing than male politicians. This means that Labor men and Coalition women are, on average, closer to the ideological centre than the other two groups: Labor women and Coalition men. (That's not to say that every female Coalition MP is to the left of every male Coalition MP – merely that the pattern holds on average.) And if you're in the centre, it seems more likely that the gender of your children might tip you in one direction or another. That is, a woman having a son is more likely to end up in the Coalition, and a man having a daughter more likely to end up in the Labor Party.

Table 2: Child gender and party preference

	AVERAGE NUMBER OF SONS	AVERAGE NUMBER OF DAUGHTERS
All parliamentarians	0.8	0.9
Male Labor parliamentarians	**0.8**	**1.1**
Female Labor parliamentarians	0.6	0.5
Male Coalition parliamentarians	1.0	1.1
Female Coalition parliamentarians	**0.7**	**0.5**

Source: Author's analysis, based on publicly available information on the children of MPs and senators in the forty-fourth parliament (based on Senate composition before July 2014). The figure for all parliamentarians includes representatives of minor parties and independents.

The differences in Table 2 are not large enough to be statistically significant, meaning it's possible that they're just a coincidence. But they are supported by work from the United States, which finds that members of Congress with daughters are more likely to cast a left-wing vote on a bill than politicians from the same party who have sons.[21] Children affect the way their legislator parents vote on defence, foreign affairs, economics, the environment, electoral regulation, social services, health and industrial relations, but the largest impact is on votes relating to reproductive rights.[22] Similar patterns have been observed in business, where CEOs with daughters pay their employees more generously, and in law, where appellate judges with daughters rule in a more feminist fashion.[23]

Looking at the effect of children's gender on their parents' behaviour highlights an issue that runs through this book – the importance of distinguishing causal effects from mere correlations. For example, if we see that student politicians are more likely to join a political party, we can't be sure that the causal effect runs from university politics to party politics. It's equally possible that the effect is the other way around, with party membership causing students to run in campus elections. Or there could be a third factor (such as having politically active parents) which causes people to get involved in university and party politics.

In thinking about luck, it's important to be sure we're identifying causal factors, rather than mere correlations. In the case of child gender, we know we're dealing with something that is effectively random. So if we see differences between parents of boys and parents of girls, we know we're observing a causal effect, rather than a mere correlation.

It might strike you as surprising that an apparently non-political factor, such as having a son or a daughter, could lead to a big political difference, such as whether you end up representing the Labor Party or the Coalition. Over recent decades, social psychologists have learned a great deal about the way that different situations can shape our views. In the 1971 Stanford Prison Experiment, twenty-four men were randomly assigned to play the roles of guards or prisoners. Within a day, the guards began to deal harshly with the prisoners. Lead researcher Philip Zimbardo writes:

> Over time, the guards became ever more abusive, and some even delighted in sadistically tormenting their prisoners. Though physical punishment was restricted, the guards on each shift were free to make up their own rules, and they invented a variety of psychological tactics to demonstrate their dominance over their powerless charges ... It is hard to imagine how a seeming game of 'cops and robbers' played by college kids, with a few academics (our research team) watching, could have descended into what became a hellhole for many in that basement. How could a mock prison, an experimental simulation, become 'a prison run by psychologists, not by the state,' in the words of one suffering prisoner? How is it possible for 'good personalities' to be so dominated by a 'bad situation'? You had to be there to believe that human character could be so swiftly transformed in a matter of days.[24]

The Stanford Prison experiment is a perfect example of circumstantial luck, in which the toss of a coin decided whether a participant was in the circumstances of a guard or a prisoner. Yet those circumstances utterly transformed people's behaviour.

◆

Throughout this chapter, I've implicitly assumed that the lucky ones are those who get into parliament. But while that might hold true of political tragics, it plainly isn't the view taken by many Australians. I've spoken with plenty of people who tell me they'd hate a job that required standing on a street corner getting abused by angry constituents, answering questions in front of a television camera, or sticking to the party line. I've also chatted with many retired politicians who look happier and more youthful as a result of stepping down from elected office.

Indeed, even those who are keen to enter politics sometimes find that failing to get preselected has unexpected upsides. In researching this book, I spoke with a candidate who came close to winning preselection for what many would regard as a 'safe seat'. Missing out was emotionally tough, but he also found that new options opened up. He took on a more challenging job and joined a corporate board. He began restoring an old vineyard – a long-held dream. Greater flexibility at work meant that he could spend more time at home with his newborn son. One weekday afternoon, he watched as his son took his first steps. In the background, Question Time was on the television. He suddenly realised that if he'd won preselection, he would not have seen his child walk for the first time. Whenever he starts to think about his 'bad luck', he told me, 'I wonder if I would really trade away the time I have enjoyed with my son.' The luck of politics runs both ways.

4

DONKEY VOTING, BEAUTY AND UNUSUAL NAMES – HOW LUCK AFFECTS INDIVIDUAL CANDIDATES

The closest federal election result in Australia took place in 1919, for the Victorian seat of Ballaraat (later renamed Ballarat). National Party candidate Edwin Kerby received 13,569 votes, defeating Labor candidate Charles McGrath, who had 13,568 votes. We often say 'every vote makes a difference', but in an Australian House of Representatives race, Kerby's 13,569 supporters are the only voters of which this is literally true. Had any one of them voted differently, it would have changed the election outcome.

Unsurprisingly, McGrath didn't see his one-vote loss as decisive, telling the media, 'This is like the first heat of a contest.'[1] He took the result to the High Court, claiming irregularities. The court overturned the result in 1920, and McGrath won the ensuing by-election.

While the Ballaraat 1919 result is the only one-vote victory in a House of Representatives election, the Senate has seen an equally tight race. In 2013, sixty-two candidates competed for Western Australia's six Senate positions. Our voting rules mean that the Australian Electoral Commission progressively eliminates the candidate with the fewest votes. As candidates are eliminated, preferences are distributed among those who remain. This means that the order in which candidates are eliminated can shape the result.

After forty-nine exclusions, the electoral commission was faced with two piles of votes of almost identical size. The smallest number of votes was held by the Australian Christians (23,531 votes), just behind the Shooters and Fishers Party (23,532 votes). As election analyst Antony Green noted at the time, the difference was critical. If the Australian Christians were eliminated, Labor won two seats and the Greens zero. But were just one vote (out of a total of 1.3 million) to change, Labor and the Greens would have one seat apiece.[2]

A one-vote margin was not the strangest thing about the 2013 Senate count. As the ballots were recounted, the Australian Electoral Commission discovered that it had lost over 1370 of them. Given the tightness of the margin, these could easily change the result. Reminiscent of what it had done nearly a century before, the High Court declared that the nation's tightest ever Senate election was void, and called a new Senate election for Western Australia. My friend Louise Pratt, the second Labor candidate, lost her job as a result.[3]

Tight Senate races in Australia are becoming increasingly common. In 1999, the Outdoor Recreation Party won a seat in the New South Wales upper house with just 0.2% of primary votes, plus preferences from twenty other parties. Glenn Druery, who masterminded the strategy, became known as 'the preference whisperer', and has since been responsible for helping the Shooters and Fishers Party win two seats in the Victorian upper house with 1.7% of the primary vote, and Ricky Muir win a Victorian Senate seat with 0.5% of the primary vote.[4] When numbers are tight, such victories require plenty of luck.

Moreover, tight contests are frequently challenged. Indeed, the stories of Ballaraat in 1919 and Western Australia in 2013 are a reminder that close elections often lead to reruns. In both those cases, the repeat election did not change the government, but sometimes close local races coincide with close numbers in the parliament as a whole.

In 1995, the Goss Labor government in Queensland was seeking a third term in office. After ending three decades of Liberal–National rule in 1989, the government expected to enjoy a lengthy tenure. But environmental issues and general dissatisfaction with the government left the election precipitously close. Goss won forty-five of the eighty-nine seats in parliament. The tightest, Mundingburra, was won by Labor candidate Ken Davies by just sixteen votes. Seizing an opportunity, the Liberal–National Coalition challenged the result on the basis that a plane from Rwanda had been delayed, preventing the votes of twenty-two military personnel being counted. A by-election was called for Mundingburra. Labor lost, and the Goss government fell.

Three years later, Queensland politics remained on a razor's edge. At that election, the anti-immigration One Nation Party won over one-fifth of the vote, and came within a single seat of holding the balance of power. A few months later, one of the One Nation members resigned his seat. Labor won the by-election, and took power again.

In the novels of Jeffrey Archer, luck sometimes decides the outcome. In *First Among Equals* (1984), protagonist Andrew

Fraser's re-election bid for the House of Commons sees him tied with a rival. The returning officer decides on a coin toss, and Fraser is returned. Similarly, in *Sons of Fortune* (2002), two brothers vie for Governor of Connecticut. When the votes are tied, a coin toss determines who will win the position. It is not hard to see luck at work in Archer's own life, which has included time served in both the House of Commons and Belmarsh Prison.

In this chapter I look at the effect of luck on individual candidates at the ballot box. I'll begin with the ultimate form of luck – the lottery used to decide ballot order – and then move on to the luck that we're dealt by our genes and our parents. Some are born male, others female. Some are born white, others black. Some are born beautiful, others of us are not. Drawing on an array of studies, I show that each of these makes a tangible difference to electability. Indeed, even a candidate's name can affect how many votes she receives.

Let's start with the phenomenon of the 'donkey vote' and its impact. For decades, a small number of voters have tended to number their ballot paper from the top downwards. Donkey voting means that the candidate listed first is more likely to win the election.

In 1901, ballot papers in federal elections were ordered alphabetically, with candidates listed in the same order as they would be in the telephone book. This meant that the higher in the alphabet you were, the higher you came on the ballot paper, and the more votes you would get. The effect was particularly strong for the Senate, where name recognition was lower and the number of candidates was larger. By 1938, 86% of senators had surnames in the first half of the alphabet.

The effect wasn't just driven by voters. Parties responded to evidence of donkey voting by refusing to preselect candidates with low-ranked names. As one commentator put it, 'citizens of the Smith, Jones or Robinson class had little hope of official recognition, the Whites and the Williams must abandon their ambitions to become senators'.[5] In one election, the first four candidates fielded by the New South Wales Labor Party had the surnames Amour, Armstrong, Arthur and Ashley.[6] All were elected.

In 1940, the Senate rules were changed so that places were assigned randomly.[7] But for House of Representatives elections, alphabetical ordering of ballot papers persisted for four decades longer. This led to the farcical situation of parties trying to outdo each other in finding candidates whose names were higher in the alphabet (much like people who call their company 'AAA Plumbing' to get the first listing in the phone book).

In the 1950s and 1960s, Australian elections were often determined by preferences from the Communist Party and the anti-communist Democratic Labor Party (DLP). Knowing that their candidates were not going to win, the parties had a high degree of flexibility in choosing who to stand. This meant that the Communist Party frequently stood candidates from the Aarons family, who as luck would have it were the leading lights of the Communist Party in Australia.[8] The DLP selected its candidates based on the name of the incumbent. For example, in the 1969 election, the DLP chose a Mr Antcliff where the sitting member was Mr Aston, and a Mr Bader where the sitting member was Mr Botsman.[9]

Alphabetical ordering was finally abolished in 1984. If you look at the phone books of that era, they are divided into A–K and L–Z. But the skew towards the first half of the alphabet was so strong that a phone book of the House of Representatives just before random ballot ordering came into effect would have split it into A–H and I–Z. Before the 1984 election, fully one-quarter of the House of Representatives had a last name starting with A, B or C.

The abolition of alphabetical ordering hasn't removed the impact of luck from elections – instead, it has distributed it in a different fashion. Today, ballot order is determined by drawing wooden balls from a rotating container – a bit like a lotto draw. It is a nailbiting ordeal for candidates and their campaign managers.

To gauge the size of the ballot-order effect, I worked with researcher Amy King – now at the Australian National University. We analysed two decades' worth of federal election results to estimate the size of the ballot-order effect in the period since randomisation.[10] Our research aimed to answer a simple question: if you're lucky enough to get pole position on the ballot paper, how many more votes do you receive?

For major party candidates, the benefit of drawing top spot on the ballot paper is a full 1 percentage point. Put another way, one in 100 voters are donkey voters, who stubbornly vote for the first person on the ballot paper. There are more donkey voters in electorates where voters are younger and there are fewer people fluent in English. And despite rising levels of education, the share of donkey voters today is about as large as it was in the 1960s. There is a lot of variation in electoral results, but our statistical analysis gives us confidence that this effect is a real difference – that it's a true signal, rather than mere noise.

Has ballot order ever changed the national result? In 1969, Gough Whitlam fell four seats short. He pointed to five seats where Labor had been disadvantaged by ballot ordering, and blamed the loss on the donkey vote. Yet as election analyst Malcolm Mackerras pointed out at the time, Whitlam had conveniently neglected to acknowledge the three seats in which Labor benefited from ballot ordering.[11] Add together the snakes and the ladders, and it doesn't look like ballot order changed the 1969 result.

But ballot ordering has changed the careers of a significant number of members of parliament. Since 1996, there have been nine candidates who drew top spot on the ballot and then won by less than 1 percentage point. My results suggest that these nine politicians can thank the luck of ballot order for their victories: Kim Beazley (ALP, 1996), Michael Lee (ALP, 1996), Ross Cameron (Lib, 1998), Gary Nairn (Lib, 1998), Paul Neville (Nat, 1998), Chris Trevor (ALP, 2007), Damien Hale (ALP, 2007), Andrew Laming (Lib, 2007) and Michelle Rowland (ALP, 2010).[12] Given that Beazley went on to serve as opposition leader in 1996–2001 and 2005–06, and given the closeness of the 2010 election, this suggests that ballot order has indeed shaped the course of Australian history.

Can we do anything about ballot order? Supporters of the current system often describe random ballot ordering as 'fair'. It is true that *before* the ballot draw, all candidates have the same chance of getting the top spot. But *after* the ballot draw, the system is manifestly unfair, since a candidate in the first position will do better than his or her rivals.

Fortunately, there is a simple solution, presently used in elections in the ACT and Tasmania. Rather than having only a single ballot paper, the Australian Electoral Commission could produce multiple versions, re-ordering the candidates each time. In this way, any ballot-order effect is shared across the candidates. This electoral system, known as Robson Rotation, produces a fairer result. And thanks to advances in printing technology, the extra cost is minimal. This is one way that we could reduce the role of luck in politics, and ensure that our electoral system better translates public opinion into parliamentary representation.

Like ballot order, your sex is the result of a tiny piece of luck. At the moment of your conception, there were millions of sperm around with X sex chromosomes, and millions with Y sex chromosomes. Pure luck determined whether you were born male or female.

And yet, if you had the luck of getting two X chromosomes, for most of Australia's history you had little chance of entering politics. The constitutional conventions that led to Federation were an all-male affair. Women were allowed to vote in Australia's first national election in 1901, but they were not permitted to stand until the second election in 1903. In the first seven decades after Federation, a total of three women were elected to the House of Representatives.

To see the effect of gender at the ballot box, Amy King and I analysed Australian elections going back to 1903.[13] Throughout this period, we found that female candidates in Australia won fewer votes than male candidates from the same party. In the 1920s, the penalty to female candidates was over 10 percentage points, making the average woman unelectable in most seats. By the 1940s, the penalty to female candidates was over 5 percentage points, making the average woman unelectable in a marginal seat. Since the 1980s, the penalty to female candidates has fallen to one-third of a percentage point, but it's still a noticeable disadvantage. Moreover, the disadvantage suffered by Australian women candidates contrasts with the advantage enjoyed by US female candidates.[14] As one woman running for election in Tennessee put it, 'A woman's place is in the House . . . and the Senate too!'[15]

The underrepresentation of women in parliament (women make up more than half of the population, but just a quarter of the members of the House of Representatives) almost certainly affects the laws parliament passes. Since female candidates are more left-wing than male candidates from the same party, overall policy outcomes are likely to become more progressive as the share of women in parliament moves towards parity. In the United States, researchers have found that state legislatures with more women pass more laws that help women, children and families, more generous workers' compensation schemes and stricter child-support enforcement policies.[16]

As noted, women candidates today are more left-wing than men. And in recent elections, women are more likely to vote for left-wing parties. Yet it wasn't always thus. When I trawled through the Australian Election Study, I was stunned to see the gender gap in the 1966 election.[17] In that election, women were 10 percentage points more likely than men to vote for the Coalition. It was hard to escape the conclusion that male voters were from Mars and female voters were from Venus. Over the following decades, the gender voting gap has steadily narrowed. Yet even in the early 1990s a difference existed. If we had banned men from voting in 1993, John Hewson would have beaten Paul Keating.

It was not until the noughties that the voting patterns of men and women had crossed over, with women becoming slightly more left-wing than men. Women have continued to shift to the left ever since – not only in Australia, but also in the United States and Western Europe.[18] Indeed, in many of those countries, women are now *much* more likely to support left-wing parties. Judging by these studies, and by the long-term trend, it seems likely that their steady shift to the left will continue.

Another factor that we are born with is our race and ethnicity.[19] Although ethnicity is not specified on the ballot paper, voters can take a guess at candidates' backgrounds from their names. To test the impact of ethnically identifiable names, I ran all federal political candidates through an algorithm known as 'OnoMAP'. The algorithm checks a vast database containing census data and other surveys from twenty-eight different countries. For any combination of first name and surname, it takes its best guess as to the ethnicity of that person, placing them into broad categories, such as English, Continental European, Asian and Muslim. The racial and ethnic estimates will not be perfect, but they are likely to mirror the impression that a voter would glean from seeing a particular name on a ballot paper.

Across Australian elections, there is some evidence that ethnically identifiable names are penalised at the ballot box. Candidates with Asian names (such as Bin Chen or Don Nguyen) do 1.5 percentage points worse. Candidates with

continental European names (for example, Willy Bach or
Teresa Farruggio) do 0.7 percentage points worse. Candidates
with Muslim names (such as Irfan Yusuf or Safwan Nasser) do
2.3 percentage points worse.

These results suggest that the luck of having a non-
Anglo name makes it harder for candidates to win elections.
Admittedly, these estimates might simply be statistical noise,
since the samples are relatively small.[20] Out of around 20,000
candidates' names, OnoMAP only codes 95 names as Asian,
732 as continental European and 67 as Muslim.

That said, these electoral findings accord with research that
I have conducted in collaboration with Alison Booth and Elena
Varganova on ethnic discrimination and low-wage jobs (we
focus on entry-level employment because the application process tends to be more streamlined).[21] By sending out thousands
of fake resumes in response to job advertisements, we were
able to test the impact of varying the applicant's name from an
Anglo name to a Chinese or Middle Eastern one. Our study
concluded that jobseekers with distinctively Middle Eastern
names had to put in 64% more applications to get the same
number of callbacks as a person with an Anglo name, while
those with Chinese names had to put in 68% more applications
to get the same number of callbacks.

Successful politicians from non-Anglo backgrounds are
understandably reluctant to speak too much about the discrimination they have experienced. But few reject the notion
that race and ethnicity matter. In the wake of Pauline Hanson's
first speech, Asian-Australian Bill O'Chee, a senator from
Queensland, drew on his childhood experiences:

In hundreds of schools around this country, young Australians watch the clock in fear as the minute hand ticks closer to lunch time. They know once they leave the safety of their classroom and enter the playground, they will become the whipping boys and whipping girls of the fear and paranoia that Mrs Hanson has whipped up. Twenty-five years ago I was one of those children.[22]

What about Indigenous candidates? There are too few Aboriginal or Torres Strait Islander candidates who have run for the national parliament to be able to estimate the impact of being Indigenous in federal elections. However, it is possible to look at the effect of being Indigenous by looking at elections in the part of Australia where racial politics has historically been sharpest: the Northern Territory.

I teamed up with psychologist Tirta Susilo (now at Dartmouth College) to look at race as a factor in Northern Territory elections.[23] Not only does the Territory have the largest share of Indigenous people, but also elections there have an interesting feature: candidates' photographs appear on the ballot paper. This fact allowed us to ask a very literal question: is voting skin-deep?

Analysing results from the 2005 Northern Territory election, we found that skin colour had a strong effect on electoral outcomes. The average electorate had about 13% Indigenous voters. In electorates with fewer Indigenous voters, candidates did better if they had lighter skin. In electorates with more Indigenous voters, candidates did better if they had darker skin.

Skin colour doesn't determine race. But when there are photos on the ballot paper, skin colour is probably the strongest indicator of a candidate's race that a voter receives. So it's hard to avoid the conclusion that electorates with relatively few Indigenous voters prefer candidates who are not identifiably Indigenous. Similarly, electorates with larger numbers of Indigenous voters tend to prefer candidates who are identifiably Indigenous. Moreover, candidates clearly consider their skin colour when deciding where to run: the eight candidates with the darkest skin colour all ran in electorates with a higher-than-average share of Indigenous voters.

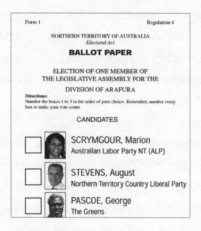

Figure 2: A sample ballot paper from the 2005 Northern Territory election (courtesy of the NT Electoral Commission)

Northern Territory political parties are clearly aware of the tendency for racial politics to shape electoral outcomes. Most famously, in the 2001 Northern Territory election, the Country Liberal Party ran both an Indigenous candidate (Phillip Alice) and a non-Indigenous candidate (John Elferink) in the central Australian seat of MacDonnell, where two-thirds of voters were Indigenous. The plan had been for Alice to attract the number 1 votes of Indigenous electors, who would then give Elferink their number 2 vote. Alice attempted to withdraw from the election in the final week of the campaign, but the ballot papers had already been printed. Elferink narrowly held onto the seat.[24]

While ballot paper photographs were originally introduced in 1980 to boost voter turnout and reduce voter error, I suspect that they have also had the inadvertent result of fostering race-based politics. The circumstantial luck of an individual's race ends up affecting how he or she performs at the ballot box.

At 185 centimetres, US president Barack Obama is 9 centimetres taller than the typical American man.[25] He is also a good deal handsomer than the typical American. In 2007, Amber Lee Ettinger posted a YouTube video titled 'I Got a Crush ... on Obama'. It garnered 23 million views.

Are taller and better-looking politicians generally more likely to be elected? Since George Washington (187 cm) took office in 1789, Americans have almost always had a president who is taller than average.[26] Moreover, taller candidates tend to beat shorter candidates. In the past thirty US presidential races, the shorter candidate won on eight occasions, while the taller candidate won on twenty occasions (in two cases, the candidates were the same height). On average, winners were 2.5 centimetres taller than losers.

But while height may matter in a US presidential race (where voters have plenty of opportunity to observe the candidates), it's possible that other dimensions of beauty matter more in regular elections. In Australia's political system, many voters will never meet the candidates. However, all of them

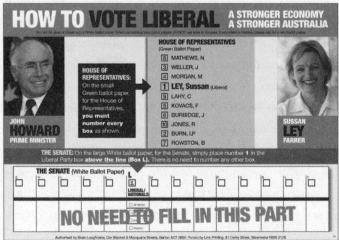

Figure 3: How-to-vote cards used in the 2004 federal election

will have the chance to see a photo of the candidate, because major parties distribute how-to-vote cards with a headshot of the candidate.

We know that candidates pay attention to the quality of their campaign photographs. Julia Gillard tells the story of campaigning outside a shopping centre, standing next to a poster displaying her name and photograph:

> This old guy comes out of the supermarket, looks at the photo, looks at me, looks at the photo, then turns back to me and says, 'Taken on a good day, was it, love?' I said, 'And you'd be bloody Robert Redford, would you, mate?'[27]

To test whether beauty affects election outcomes, Amy King and I obtained the photographs used on the how-to-vote cards of all major party candidates in the 2004 federal election.[28] To avoid any suggestion of bias, we employed independent 'beauty raters', and asked each of them to rate candidates' beauty on a scale from 1 (least beautiful) to 10 (most beautiful). We used two teams of raters – an Australian team and an American team. The Australians were more representative of the electorate, but might have recognised some of the candidates. The Americans were less representative, but had the advantage that none of them recognised a single Australian politician.

It turns out that it doesn't matter who does the rating, because most people have the same notions of beauty.[29] People tend to be rated as more beautiful if they smile, and if their faces are more symmetrical. Most of us regard strong features on men as more handsome, and fine features on women as more attractive. To put it bluntly, beauty is *not* in the eye of the beholder. A two-month-old baby will stare longer at an attractive person than an unattractive person.[30] Indeed, there's even a website – symmeter.com – where you can upload a photograph of yourself and have it rated for symmetry, which closely matches what most people associate with beauty.

On average, beauty turned out to be an extremely strong predictor of how many votes a candidate received. For example, suppose that we compare a candidate of average beauty with a candidate in the top 15%, a member of the 'beauty elite'. In this match-up, the more beautiful candidate can expect to win an additional 1 to 2 percentage points of the vote than the average-looking candidate. Since one in ten electoral races are decided by a margin this small, this makes beauty politically important. Fully one-tenth of Australian electoral results could be changed by the choice of a particularly beautiful (or particularly ugly) candidate. As one journalist put it: 'MEMO: all spunkrats. Ever thought of making a run for political office?'[31]

Not everyone was delighted by our results. *Herald Sun* scribbler Andrew Bolt excoriated the research on his blog, and then added, 'As they judge, let them be judged. Leigh and King are pictured below.'[32] The comments from his readers left no doubt that I was the less comely co-author.

Around the same time Amy King and I carried out our study, two other teams were investigating the same issue. It turns out that in both German and Finnish elections, better-looking candidates win more votes.[33] Finnish voters are more likely to be swayed by beauty than Australian voters, while German voters are less influenced by looks. Yet one curious finding stands out: in those countries, beauty has a larger effect on *female candidates*, while in Australia, beauty has a larger effect on *male candidates*. Amy King and I speculated that one reason for this might be an Australian stereotype that causes some people to regard attractive women as less competent. For example, 'dumb blonde' jokes are more likely to be directed at women than at men.

But for both male and female candidates, overall, good looks are rewarded at the ballot box. While Senator John McCain may have described Washington, DC, as 'Hollywood for ugly people', the evidence from each of these studies suggests that a pleasing physical appearance is positively correlated with electoral performance. One breakfast radio presenter asked me whether our results could really be believed, given the number of less-than-gorgeous individuals in the Australian House of Representatives. I answered honestly: 'Mate, you should have seen the ones who missed out.'

The effect of beauty in politics mirrors results in other fields. In the Australian labour market, Jeff Borland and I have shown that men rated 'above average' for attractiveness had household incomes that were 15% higher, while those rated 'below average' had household incomes 25% lower. In fact, not only do beautiful people earn more, they are also more effective in collecting charitable donations and perform better on television game shows.[34] In the courtroom, beautiful defendants are more likely to be acquitted, while uglier people are more likely to be judged criminals.[35] There is also some evidence that unattractive people tend to choose occupations where they can be judged primarily on their writings. My friend Richard Holden notes that many Nobel-winning economists tend to be short in stature. Indeed, the economists who shaped mid-twentieth-century Australian economic policy were known as 'the seven dwarfs'.[36]

There are two possible reasons why looks might matter in politics. One is that voters are looking to choose the most effective representative and regard looks as an important part of what makes a successful politician. Perhaps they think that good grooming is a marker of a well-organised personality. Maybe they regard someone who is handsome as more capable of engaging an audience. An economist might think of this as a 'productivity' explanation.

Another possibility is that the beauty effect is a marker of voters' disengagement from the political process. Uninterested in the issues and uninspired by the parties, they respond by voting for the spunkrat. In this explanation, the beauty effect looks less like a reward for high productivity and more like what economists might call discrimination.

To separate these two explanations, Amy King and I looked at whether the political 'beauty premium' was constant across electorates (as the productivity explanation might imply) or was higher in places with more apathetic voters (as the discrimination theory suggests). We found that the beauty premium is larger in those electorates where more people say that they are not interested in the election, and do not care who wins. This suggests that the political beauty effect is more likely to be due to discrimination than productivity.

The beauty effect fits into what psychologists have referred to as 'thin slicing': our tendency to make snap judgements based on a small amount of information. When we know very little about someone, their physical beauty matters a lot, but as we come to know them, other factors become more important. An alluring smile might set your heart racing when you first meet the love of your life, but that same smile is unlikely to win an argument after a decade of marriage. In a Westminster system, where leaders are chosen by their colleagues rather than being directly elected as in presidential systems, there's little evidence that looks matter for the top job.

And yet appearance still seems to matter for junior politicians. According to a recent Israeli study, good-looking members of the Knesset received considerably more television coverage than their uglier counterparts.[37] With visual media playing a more significant role than ever before in Australian politics, this suggests that the beauty premium in Australian politics might grow larger over time.

To some extent, people can control their appearance. When they analysed Australian election photographs using facial recognition software, a team of Japanese researchers concluded that candidates with bigger smiles won more votes.[38] But to the extent that good looks are the result of genes rather than self-presentation, there is an argument that we should worry a little more about the finding that beautiful candidates win more votes.

Indeed, University of Texas economist Dan Hamermesh has argued that if beauty is in the genes, then we should think of discrimination against unattractive people as similar to discrimination against women and racial minorities.[39] Hamermesh points out that sex, race and beauty are all characteristics that people are born with. In this sense, having symmetrical or asymmetrical facial features is as much out of your control as whether you have a Y chromosome or a particular skin colour.

And then there's the name your parents choose to give you. A surprising body of research finds correlations between someone's name and their life outcomes. In love, consumer choices and residential decisions, individuals seem drawn to people, products and places that remind them of their own names. This subconscious egoism can have life-changing effects. As one study sums it up, 'Toby is more likely to buy a Toyota, move to Toronto, and marry Tonya than is Jack, who instead is more likely to buy a Jaguar, move to Jacksonville, and marry Jackie.'[40] Other researchers have shown that the impact of names carries through to career choices. For example, people named Dennis or Denise are overrepresented among dentists.[41] Alas for Dennis the dentist, there is also some evidence that people whose names start with 'D' tend to die earlier.[42]

When psychologists delve into name effects, they have found that people like the letter that their name starts with. For example, Zelma is more likely to prefer the letter Z to the letter S.[43] This tends to be mostly harmless – though not always. In the United States, where letter grades are commonly used in schools, students whose names start with A and B are more likely to get high grades than students whose names start with C and D.[44]

Why might people with common names do better in politics? Several studies find that people are more generous to those with a similar name, and find them more likeable. In the 2000 US presidential campaign, people whose surnames started with B were more likely to give money to George W. Bush, while those whose surnames began with G were more likely to contribute to Al Gore.[45] Similarly, respondents are more willing to return a survey if the researcher's name is like theirs.[46] When given a hypothetical scenario in which the main character's name is close to theirs, people are more likely to say that they would help out.

With the advent of the internet, most of us have found people around the world who share our names. My most famous Googlegängers are Andrew Leigh the Los Angeles screenwriter, Andrew Leigh the London management writer, and Andrew Leigh the Irish jockey. As Stanford's Jeremy Bailenson puts it, 'Self-similarity is really one of the largest driving forces of behaviour of social beings. When someone is similar to you, you give them special privileges.'[47] This might extend to buying something from them, or even voting for them. Because common names are shared by more voters, it is reasonable to think that having one might be an asset in politics.

Parents spend considerable time choosing a name for their child – sometimes even going so far as to engage a professional name consultant.[48] This may explain the rise in unusual names over recent years. Since the 1950s, the share of babies given a name that was in the top ten for that year has steadily declined.[49] In the early 1950s, 37% of boys and 26% of girls were given a name that was in the top ten that year (names such as Gary, David, Helen and Susan). But in recent years, top ten names (such as James, William, Emily and Sienna) only accounted for 13% of boys and 11% of girls.

But while parents put plenty of thought into what to name their children, few think much about the *electoral* impact of that name. I would hazard a guess that few think about the possibility that their child will end up running for office. If your name is electorally attractive, it's probably a surprise to your parents. So from the point of view of seeking political office, names can be thought of as a form of luck.

Let's start with a simple look at the names of political candidates. Using a dataset of all candidates who ran in elections from 1901 to 2013, I asked the question: which names are used significantly more by Coalition than Labor candidates? For each first name, I counted up the number of times it was used by candidates from each side of politics, counting each individual only once (so the data was not skewed towards those who ran for office many times). Naturally, we don't expect the proportions to be precisely the same across parties, but I was looking for major differences – those that social scientists call statistically significant.[50]

Table 3 reports the names that are significantly more common among Coalition candidates. For certain names, the partisan difference is very large. The names Alex, Billy, Bruce, Don, Philip and Roy are ten times more likely to belong to Coalition candidates than to Labor candidates. Other names that are significantly more common among Coalition candidates are Bronwyn, Henry, Jonathan, Kay and Trish.

Table 3: Coalition names

FIRST NAME	FREQUENCY AMONG COALITION CANDIDATES (%)	FREQUENCY AMONG ALP CANDIDATES (%)	RATIO
Alan	1.54	0.74	2.1
Alex	0.29	0.02	13.4
Alexander	1.09	0.24	4.6
Allen	0.29	0.09	3.4
Athol	0.21	0.02	9.8
Billy	0.37	0.02	17.1
Bronwyn	0.19	0.02	8.6
Bruce	1.62	0.11	14.9
Denis	0.35	0.09	4.0
Dennis	0.27	0.07	4.1

FIRST NAME	FREQUENCY AMONG COALITION CANDIDATES (%)	FREQUENCY AMONG ALP CANDIDATES (%)	RATIO
Don	0.40	0.02	18.3
Donald	1.17	0.54	2.2
Edmund	0.24	0.04	5.5
Eric	0.82	0.26	3.2
Geoffrey	0.61	0.20	3.1
Harold	0.74	0.39	1.9
Henry	1.30	0.72	1.8
Howard	0.16	0.02	7.3
Ian	1.33	0.26	5.1
Jeff	0.16	0.02	7.3
Jonathan	0.16	0.02	7.3
Kay	0.21	0.04	4.9
Ken	0.35	0.04	7.9
Kevin	0.90	0.39	2.3
Malcolm	0.64	0.07	9.8
Peter	3.40	2.20	1.5
Phil	0.32	0.07	4.9
Philip	0.98	0.07	15.1
Phillip	0.29	0.07	4.5
Roy	0.29	0.02	13.4
Russell	0.48	0.11	4.4
Stanley	0.40	0.09	4.6
Trish	0.24	0.07	3.7
Wallace	0.16	0.02	7.3
Walter	0.66	0.17	3.8

Table 4 carries out the same exercise for Labor names. The names Clyde, Cyril, Gilbert, Kim and Laurie are each at least ten times more common among Labor than Coalition candidates. Other names that are significantly more common among Labor candidates are Carolyn, Helen, James, Simon and Steve.

Table 4: Labor names

FIRST NAME	FREQUENCY AMONG ALP CANDIDATES (%)	FREQUENCY AMONG COALITION CANDIDATES (%)	RATIO
Albert	0.91	0.35	2.6
Benjamin	0.20	0.03	7.4
Bernie	0.20	0.03	7.4
Carolyn	0.17	0.03	6.5
Clyde	0.33	0.03	12.3
Con	0.17	0.03	6.5
Cyril	0.35	0.03	13.1
Daniel	0.61	0.11	5.7
Edgar	0.20	0.03	7.4
Edward	1.89	0.90	2.1
Francis	1.28	0.45	2.8
Frank	1.52	0.37	4.1
Gilbert	0.28	0.03	10.6
Harry	0.50	0.21	2.4
Helen	0.17	0.03	6.5
Herbert	0.63	0.13	4.7
James	3.26	2.50	1.3
Jenny	0.30	0.05	5.7
Joseph	1.50	0.37	4.0
Kim	0.67	0.03	25.4
Lance	0.26	0.05	4.9
Laurie	0.46	0.03	17.2
Leo	0.39	0.05	7.4

FIRST NAME	FREQUENCY AMONG ALP CANDIDATES (%)	FREQUENCY AMONG COALITION CANDIDATES (%)	RATIO
Leonard	0.57	0.25	2.4
Lindsay	0.24	0.05	4.5
Martin	0.48	0.11	4.5
Norman	0.80	0.29	2.8
Ralph	0.48	0.08	6.0
Ronald	0.52	0.24	2.2
Rowland	0.17	0.03	6.5
Simon	0.24	0.05	4.5
Steve	0.41	0.13	3.1
Thomas	2.09	1.17	1.8

Some Coalition-skewed names are traditional English names (Edmund, Philip/Phillip, Wallace), while some Labor-skewed names are Irish (Bernie, Frank, Francis, Joseph). In one case, the difference is one of formality, with the name Harold being twice as popular among Coalition candidates, but Harry twice as common among Labor candidates.

How does a candidate's name affect his or her performance at the ballot box? Earlier in this chapter, I discussed one clear factor: in the years before ballot ordering was randomised, having a surname higher in the alphabet was a significant electoral advantage.

But that's not the only way names might matter. Let's start with the effect of having a more common first name. Candidates with popular names might do better because they seem more familiar to voters – perhaps even subconsciously reminding them of a friend or family member. Names like Julie and John are more familiar to most of us than Elissa and Edwin.

To test the effect of name popularity, I analysed a dataset of names given to babies born in New South Wales over half a century.[51] Lo and behold, I found that those with more popular names performed better. A 1% increase in the popularity of a name leads to a 0.3 percentage point boost at the ballot box.

What does this mean in practice? Suppose we take candidates with the most common first names: Michael, David, Peter, John, Matthew, Jessica, Jennifer, Michelle, Sarah and Rebecca. These names are given to between 1% and 3% of all babies of that sex. Now, let's take another set of candidates with unusual names, such as Tobias, Brody, Gareth, Giovanni, Seth, Nina, Kristine, Leigh, Eleanor and Gina. (These names are given to less than 0.1% of babies of that sex.) Because the first set of names feels more familiar to voters, they garner up to 1 percentage point more of the vote. In a tight marginal seat, that could be the difference between victory and defeat.

This result bookends another finding from the academic literature on first names: that juveniles convicted of a crime tend to have unusual names (such as Adriaan, Kareem or Preston).[52] It seems that while uncommon names are more likely to see you in jail, common names are more likely to end you up in parliament.[53]

Complex names also have an impact. For example, candidates with longer surnames do worse at the ballot box. Add another ten characters to a candidate's surname, and he or she loses 1.6 percentage points of the vote. Mere name length suggests that those who ran with last names like Bassingthwaighte, Squillacciotti and Chandrasegaran will average nearly 2 percentage points fewer votes than those with last names like Roy, Bell and Short.

The problem is worst for those with hyphenated surnames, such as Rowland-Hornblow, Montefiore-Castle and Sheffield-Brotherton. On average, candidates with hyphenated surnames do 2.3 percentage points worse. Mostly, this is because they're twice the length of the average surname, but there is some suggestive evidence that Australian voters punish hyphenated surnames in themselves.

If long names and hyphenated names are indeed an electoral disadvantage, we might expect to see more complex names in the Senate (where candidates run on party lists) than the House. Indeed, senators have longer surnames than MPs.[54] It also turns out that there are three senators with hyphenated surnames, but no members of the House of Representatives with hyphenated surnames.

The number of names matters too. Some candidates list their middle names on the ballot paper, while others do not (either because they do not have a middle name, or because they opt for simplicity). Those who list their middle names do 0.4 percentage points worse overall.

Nobody chooses their name with an eye to getting elected. Well, almost nobody. With the possible exception of the person who changed his name to 'Prime Minister John Piss The Family Court and Legal Aid' to run against Prime Minister Howard in 1998, our names are chosen for us by our parents. It's true that some women change their surnames after getting married, but it's hard to imagine that these choices are often, if ever, made to improve their chances of winning public office.

The name you're given is a form of luck – and like other forms of luck, it shapes how you perform at the ballot box. In a tight election, familiar first names, short surnames and surnames without hyphens are more likely to lead to electoral success. Some politicians have won despite their unlucky names, such as current Alabama treasurer 'Young Boozer' (campaign slogan: 'Funny Name – Serious Leadership'). But in general, voters prefer candidates with simple and familiar names.

Then, just when you think you've won election, there's the unpredictability of how the High Court will interpret the Constitution. In 1992, the High Court surprised many when it ruled that independent member Phil Cleary had breached the Constitution by failing to resign as a Victorian school teacher. Although Cleary was only on the casual list for the education department, the court decided that this was enough to constitute an 'office of profit under the crown'. Four years later, Liberal member Jackie Kelly was caught by the same provision. She had been an air force officer at the time of nominating (though not on election day), and the High Court ruled her election invalid.

Both Cleary and Kelly were unlucky to have their careers disrupted by the High Court, but eventually won re-election with increased majorities. Others were not so lucky. Consider the case of Nuclear Disarmament Party candidate Robert Wood. Having taken his place in the Senate in August 1987, Wood innocently applied for a passport. It was then discovered that although his parents had brought him from England to Australia in 1963, he had never taken out Australian citizenship. After the High Court ruled against him, a recount gave the seat to the number two candidate on Wood's ticket: Irina Dunn. Dunn was asked to resign the seat in favour of Wood, but refused.

In the 1998 election, Queenslander Heather Hill won a seat in the Senate for the One Nation Party. Like Wood, she was born in the UK. Unlike Wood, she had taken out Australian citizenship. But Hill had failed to renounce her British citizenship, and the Constitution says that anyone with allegiance to a 'foreign power' is ineligible to be a senator. By a vote of four to three, the High Court decided that it had jurisdiction to hear the case. A majority of judges concluded that although Britain was not a foreign power when the Constitution was written, by 1999 it had become a foreign power.

A recount gave the Senate seat to One Nation's second candidate, Len Harris. Proving that right-wing parties are no less dastardly than left-wing ones, he refused to give up the seat for Hill. The year after the election, he sacked her as a staff member. Within a year, a one-vote margin on the High Court had seen Heather Hill go from being senator-elect to jobless.

In 1990, independent Ted Mack ran for the federal seat of North Sydney. Mack had previously served in state and local government, and his profile ensured that he easily defeated incumbent Liberal MP John Spender.

Six years later, Mack retired, on the basis that if he stayed in federal politics for a third term, he would be eligible for a parliamentary pension, which he did not want. His successor was Joe Hockey. Had Mack not taken a principled stance against parliamentary pensions, it's unlikely Hockey would have entered parliament when he did, and it's likely that someone else would today be the treasurer of Australia.

Adam Bandt had similar good fortune. He ran for the seat

of Melbourne in the 2007 election, but was unable to unseat Labor's Lindsay Tanner. Then in June 2010, just two months from polling day, Tanner suddenly announced his resignation. Bandt went from underdog to favourite. With preferences from the Liberal Party, he won the seat for the Greens.

After polling day came another stroke of good luck. Tight numbers in the House of Representatives gave Bandt more influence, and brought him into the public spotlight. In the 2013 election, the Liberal Party did not preference Bandt, but his high profile meant that he was re-elected nonetheless. Bandt worked hard, but hard work hadn't been enough in 2007. Nor did hard work save Michael Organ, who won the seat of Cunningham for the Greens in 2002, but lost it two years later.

Luck matters at the ballot box in quirky and unexpected ways. According to one study, members of the US Congress tend to have been relatively old for their school year – a pattern that can also be seen in sports stars.[55] Unless you think that hard work can shape your birthdate, that's chance at work.

For individuals running for election in Australia, the circumstances of your birth shape your likely success. Women tend to get fewer votes than men, while people with traditional English names do better than those with Continental European, Asian or Muslim names. Being bestowed a shorter surname or a more common first name by your parents makes you more electable. Being top of the ballot boosts your vote, as does the luck of facial symmetry – also known as beauty.

But luck doesn't just affect individual races – it can also help decide who forms government. So let's move now from candidates to parties, and see how luck can shape election outcomes.

5

WEATHER, SHARKS AND THE WORLD ECONOMY – HOW LUCK AFFECTS POLITICAL PARTIES

In the summer of 1916, a series of shark attacks on the New Jersey shore killed four people, including an eleven-year-old boy (the attacks inspired the film *Jaws*). A few months later, Americans voted in a presidential election. As a careful academic analysis has shown, the vote for the incumbent president (Woodrow Wilson) was around 10 percentage points lower in New Jersey's beachside counties.[1] Although most voters probably knew that the president was powerless to prevent shark attacks, they wanted to punish someone.

President Wilson's administration was not the first government to be blamed for an event outside its control. In Egypt, pharaohs were seen as having divine responsibility for making the Nile flood annually.[2] If the river did not flood, their reign was shortened. Similarly, Maya kings were seen as responsible for good harvest rains, and a drought regarded as 'tantamount to the breaking of a royal promise'.[3] When Krakatoa exploded in 1883, local missionaries blamed the Dutch colonists.[4]

Indeed, the propensity to blame others for natural events

can even lead to violence. When a 'little ice age' caused harvests to fail in the late 1600s and early 1700s, there was an upsurge in witch trials across Europe.[5] In one German town, 400 women – mostly poor widows – were killed in a single day. In modern-day Tanzania, the pattern holds: more extreme weather conditions increase the number of witch murders.[6] Other research has shown that black lynchings in the United States were more frequent when land and cotton values fell.[7]

With Australian National University economist Paul Burke, I analysed the impact of bad weather on democratic change.[8] Analysing data for 154 countries over the past half-century, we found that temperature and rainfall shocks reduced economic growth, which in turn increased the likelihood of a transition from autocracy to democracy. When poor weather causes an economic recession, the chances of a dictator being ousted are three times as high. Other researchers have found a link between regime change and floods, earthquakes and windstorms.[9]

What about the weather on election day? To test the effect, I collected historical weather data across Australia on federal election days, and compared it with the two-party preferred vote that the incumbent party received in a particular state or territory. The results are not quite as powerful as in developing nations, but they do suggest that weather matters. If it rains, the incumbent party does 1.6 percentage points better than they would normally do in that state. Conversely, if the temperature is 10° Celsius hotter than usual for that state, the incumbent party sees a 1.8 percentage point fall in its vote.[10]

Repeating the analysis with state election data points in a similar direction: incumbent parties do better with a bit of rain. If you're running for re-election, pray for wet and cool. If you're attempting to unseat a government, hope for dry and hot. Weather that boils the blood seems to make for angry voters.

Interestingly, the effects don't seem partisan – what matters is the party in power, not its ideological complexion. This contrasts with evidence for countries with voluntary voting systems, where progressive parties (such as the US Democrats) find it harder to get their voters to the polls if it rains on election day.[11] In Australia, weather matters, but through its impact on the national psyche, rather than because it affects turnout.

We tend to think it unfair that governments should be punished for sun and drought. But when it comes to economic performance, most people would regard it as reasonable to penalise governments that have presided over recessions. And yet for a small economy enmeshed in a global system, a serious slump can be as much out of your control as a shark attack.

To test the effect of the global economic cycle on election results, I studied over 200 national elections. For each, I asked the questions: how was the world economy performing, and how was the country performing *relative* to the world economy? If they are acting rationally, voters should ignore the former and reward the latter. But I found that when the world economy boomed, national leaders were more likely to be re-elected, even if their country's relative performance was mediocre.[12] If you're a world leader facing re-election, each additional percentage point of world economic growth raises your chances of getting back into office by 7 percentage points. By contrast, each additional percentage point of national growth – relative to the world economy – boosts re-election chances by only 3 percentage points, less than half as much.

If we regard world growth as luck, and national growth (relative to world growth) as competence, this result suggests that voters give twice as much weight to luck as to competence. When you think about it, this doesn't make much sense. Why do Belgian voters reward their government when the world economy is booming and punish their government when the world economy is in a funk?

The same failure to benchmark can be seen in state elections. Australian expatriate economist Justin Wolfers has shown that state governors in the manufacturing heartland of the United States are more likely to be re-elected when oil prices are high, and more likely to be turfed out of office when the oil price falls.[13] Since governors have no control over the oil price, this looks a lot like blaming the messenger.

It turns out that Australian voters in state elections behave in a similar fashion. Last time I checked, the Tasmanian government had little influence over the unemployment rate in the United States. Yet it might want to keep an eye on Wall Street, since the American economy has historically had a large impact on whether Australian state governments get re-elected. Analysing nearly 200 Australian state elections, Mark McLeish and I found that state governments were significantly more likely to be re-elected when the American economy was strong than when it was in recession.[14] Raise the US unemployment rate by 1 percentage point, and the odds of an Australian state government being re-elected fall by 3 to 4 percentage points.[15]

From 1992 to 1995, six of Australia's eight states and territories ousted their government. But in the early 2000s, state elections almost invariably saw the incumbent returned. The orthodox political narrative is that early 1990s governments led by Joan Kirner and Michael Field were incompetent, while early 2000s governments led by Steve Bracks and Peter Beattie were highly adroit.

When we bring luck into it, the picture looks different. Yes, the governments led by Bracks and Beattie were talented, but they had the great strength of governing at a time when the world economy was booming. And, sure, the Kirner and Field governments had their limitations (who doesn't?), but we're missing a significant part of the story if we ignore the fact that the world economy was in an economic slump in the early 1990s.

During the 2006 South Australian election, Prime Minister John Howard told a radio interviewer:

> One of the things I can do is point out immediately that during this election campaign, Mr Rann will undoubtedly say how strong the South Australian economy is and claim all of the credit. But most people, when they step back and think about it, realise that the strength of the economy is determined by national economic policy ... And I would hope that South Australian voters would keep that in mind and put aside the more extravagant claims that are going to be made by Mr Rann during his campaign.[16]

John Howard was half-right. During the mid-2000s, the strength of the South Australian economy was partly due to national factors. But what he failed to tell listeners was that, in turn, the strength of the Australian economy was due to world factors. 2006 was a cracker year for global growth, and Australia was sharing in that success. Rann might have been fortunate, but Howard had been sharing in the same luck for much of his prime ministership.

Economic luck has not been equally shared across the political spectrum. As journalist Laura Tingle points out, 'It has been a truism of Australian politics for decades that the Coalition has traditionally been blessed with good economic luck, while Labor has tended to be voted into office just as things have turned sour: the OPEC oil crisis in the early 1970s in the case of Whitlam; the "banana republic" fall in the terms of trade, and subsequent sharp reversal, for Hawke and Keating; the global financial crisis for Rudd.'[17] Tingle might also have added to her list the Scullin Labor government, sworn in two days before the stock market crash, and the Curtin Labor government, elected two months before Pearl Harbor.

In more recent times, the pattern has persisted. As economics commentator Alan Kohler noted just before the 2013 election: 'If the ALP loses this year it can count itself very unlucky indeed: the Rudd/Gillard/Rudd Government will have exactly encompassed the second-biggest crash and world recession in history followed by the slowest, most difficult recovery. Compare that with John Howard, who, after winning that 2001 election, governed during one of the great economic booms in history, escaping into satisfied retirement 24 days after the stock market peaked.'[18] As Kohler points out, Julia Gillard's prime ministership almost perfectly coincided with a boom in the Australian dollar. The high dollar was partly driven by US monetary policy, and placed considerable stress on Australian industries such as domestic tourism and manufacturing. Gillard's prime ministership would not have been trouble-free had the dollar been lower, but it certainly didn't help.

Until now, this chapter has focused on the kinds of luck that can cause parties to win or lose an election. But electoral fortunes can also be more idiosyncratic. In recent years, researchers seeking to explain voting behaviour have moved from looking purely at 'rational' factors such as household finances, leadership perception and campaign issues, to look at more unexpected forces such as emotional appeal and family background.

One such strand of research looks at the impact of child gender on voting behaviour. Recall from Chapter 3 that male Labor parliamentarians are more likely to have daughters, while female Coalition parliamentarians are more likely to have sons. In other countries, researchers have applied a similar technique, but looking at the children of voters rather than parliamentarians. A study that looked at Germany and the United Kingdom found that parents with daughters were more likely to be left-wing than parents with sons.[19] Conversely, a US study found that parents with daughters were more likely to be right-wing.[20] A third such study – combining data for thirty-six European countries – found no relationship whatsoever between child gender and voter behaviour.[21]

Given that the international evidence is mixed, let's look at Australia. To test this, I searched the archives for a dataset that included information on the gender of children and their parents' party preference. Eventually, I found a survey from the 1980s. To keep things simple, I focused on the gender of the firstborn child and asked the question: are you more likely to support the Coalition if your first child is a boy?

Table 5: Child gender and party preference

	FIRSTBORN IS A SON	FIRSTBORN IS A DAUGHTER
Male voters	46% ALP / 54% Coalition	55% ALP / 45% Coalition
Female voters	50% ALP / 50% Coalition	48% ALP / 52% Coalition
All voters	48% ALP / 52% Coalition	51% ALP / 49% Coalition

As the results in Table 5 demonstrate, child gender matters, but only for male voters.[22] Men whose firstborn is a son had a 54% chance of supporting the Coalition, while men with a firstborn daughter had only a 45% chance of backing the Coalition. Given that the difference is 9 percentage points, this provides statistically significant evidence that one in eleven men became Coalition and not Labor supporters because of the gender of their children. Since child gender is a matter of luck, we know that the effect is causal.

Admittedly, the Australian survey on child gender and partisan preference is now more than a generation old, so it's possible that the effect may not be as strong today. And yet, if there is an effect of child gender on voting preference, it would be another example of luck at work. Whether your firstborn is male or female is entirely random, and yet it appears to have shifted the voting patterns of one-eleventh of Australian men – at least in the 1980s. You've probably seen the bumper sticker 'Insanity is hereditary – you get it from your kids'. Perhaps the same goes for political attitudes.

The way in which children affect parents' attitudes is through socialisation. For example, one study suggests that in a world where women suffer pay discrimination, single women are likely to prefer more government intervention than single men.[23] So a father of daughters might be more inclined to support a more activist government (and therefore more left-wing parties) than a father of sons. We could tell similar stories about progressive taxes, Medicare and government pensions – all of which benefit women more than men. In other words, the genes that a father passes on to his children might come back to shape his world view, and perhaps even how he votes.

Another fascinating piece of research suggests that the luck of genetic selection might directly shape a person's political views. In a recent study, over 13,000 Australians were asked their view on topics such as privatisation, the death penalty, trade unions, private schools and defence spending.[24] The researchers then used these to form a left–right scale. They sequenced each person's genes, and analysed how genes mapped against political views. The research team found several sets of genes that are correlated with political attitudes. These genes relate to neurotransmitter functioning, including serotonin and glutamic acid, which shape generous and aggressive thoughts. Other researchers suggest that the genes that affect our dopamine receptor might shape our political preferences.[25] With over 20,000 genes in the human genome, it will take more follow-up studies before researchers can confidently claim that they have found the 'voting gene'. But given the many ways that genes affect us, it does seem plausible that they also have an impact on political attitudes.

For political candidates, we already know genes affect political outcomes through gender, ethnicity and beauty. But as geneticists explore the biology of ideology, we are likely to learn more about how the luck of our genes shapes our voting preferences.

♠

On 11 March 2004, militants packed more than 100 kilograms of dynamite into thirteen backpack bombs, and placed them onto four commuter trains taking passengers into central Madrid. Each backpack contained concentrated explosives, stolen from a mining operation, plus a mobile phone, with its alarm set for 7.37 am.

The bombs detonated with horrific force. One explosion was so powerful that it ripped the train in two. Bodies were sent flying. Some victims were burned to death in their seats. In the two minutes it took the bombs to detonate, 191 people were killed, and nearly 2000 injured. Amet Oulabid, a 23-year-old carpenter who got off one of the trains just before the explosions, recalls: 'There was a security guard dripping with blood. People were pushing and running. I saw a woman who had fallen on the tracks because people were pushing so hard. I escaped with my life by a hair.'[26] It was the worst terrorist attack in Spain's history.

The response of the Spanish government was swift. 'It is absolutely clear,' said the interior minister, 'that the terrorist organization ETA was seeking an attack with wide repercussions.'[27] But it soon became clear that ETA, a Basque separatist organisation, had not carried out the bombings. Instead, it had been carried out by an al-Qaeda–inspired terrorist cell. Many Spaniards saw José Aznar's conservative government as seeking to mislead them. Three days after the election, Spain went to the polls and ousted the Aznar government. Its mistaken response to the Madrid bombings is regarded as one of the main reasons for the result.

Like shark attacks and hot days, the brutality of a terrorist attack can shape an election outcome. In the lead-up to the 2001 Australian election, betting market data made it possible to track – on a daily basis – the odds that the Howard government would win re-election.[28] The day before the shocking 11 September terrorist attacks, the probability was assessed as just 35%. A week afterwards, it had risen to 45%. It may seem callous to consider the political repercussions of terrorist attacks, but if we ignore them we risk missing an important part of the political picture. Like the rest of us, governments and political parties are buffeted by unforeseen events.

While some events shape election outcomes, others have a more idiosyncratic effect. Male voters with daughters appear to be more left-wing, while new research suggests that genetics can be mapped against political orientation. Another study shows that having time to think can sway the result. When people are distracted by other tasks, they are more likely to support conservative ideas. This suggests that on polling day, a busy voter rushing between dropping the kids at soccer and doing the shopping is more likely to vote for the conservative candidate.[29] Unless there is an overall upsurge in busyness on election day, this is unlikely to change the result – but it is another reminder of the role that chance plays in the political process.

Having discussed luck as it affects candidates and parties, I now turn to the most challenging job of all: leadership. How does luck affect someone's ability to win – and hold – a leadership position?

6

HEART ATTACKS, CLOSE VOTES AND THE SHARE MARKET – THE LUCK OF LEADERS

In mid-2009, it was clear that Malcolm Turnbull's leadership of the Liberal Party was in trouble. A Treasury official with the Dickensian name of Godwin Grech had been secretly leaking valuable information to Turnbull. But then Grech overreached, fabricating an email from the prime minister's office. On the basis of the email, Turnbull accused Prime Minister Kevin Rudd of being corrupt and lying to parliament. When the truth was revealed, Turnbull's personal approval rating suffered the largest drop of any opposition leader in a quarter of a century.[1] The survey was accompanied by the subheading: 'Moves against leader under way'.

A few months later, on 24 November, the Liberal Party debated whether the Coalition should support the Labor government's emissions trading scheme. In order to move himself up the speaking order, Andrew Robb, who had recently returned from leave after suffering from depression, passed Turnbull a note saying, 'the side-effects of the medication I am on now make me very tired. I'd be really grateful if you could get me to my feet soon.'[2] Robb later wrote that he 'could have easily sat there for another couple of hours,' but defended his actions on the basis that if Turnbull had known what was coming, he would have put Robb last on the speaking list. Robb excoriated the policy, and received a standing ovation. Turnbull was furious, but the damage was done.

As the leadership contenders jostled, attitudes to the emissions trading scheme became pivotal. On 27 November, Joe Hockey tweeted, 'Hey team re The ETS. Give me your views please on the policy and political debate. I really want your feedback.' The spectacle of a senior politician asking Twitter how best to address climate change led to public ridicule and raised questions as to whether Hockey was up to leading the party.

On 30 November, a group of senior Liberals – including Tony Abbott, Peter Dutton, Joe Hockey, Nick Minchin, Christopher Pyne and Liberal Party director Brian Loughnane – met to discuss who would replace Turnbull.[3] It was agreed Hockey would run, and that if he won, party members would be allowed a free vote on the emissions trading scheme. As the meeting broke up, Abbott paused with his hand on the office door handle, turned back to the room and said, 'Ah, ah, I think I will have a go, sorry.' Then he left the room.

The next day – an unseasonably cold Canberra morning – the Liberal party room voted on the three leadership contenders.[4] Tony Abbott got the most votes, and Malcolm Turnbull (with 26 votes) narrowly eliminated Joe Hockey (with 23 votes). The way the maths of ballots works is that each person who switches changes the margin by two (one candidate loses a vote, while another gains a vote). So if two Turnbull supporters had backed Hockey instead, Hockey would have stayed in the race. As Hockey put it afterwards, 'There's always a surprise in these ballots, I had one today'.[5] Perhaps if Hockey hadn't turned to Twitter for advice on climate change, he might have garnered those two additional votes.

In the final round, it was down to Abbott and Turnbull. If all Liberal Party members had voted, the ballot would have been tied. But there was a hitch. On the weekend before the ballot, Turnbull supporter Fran Bailey was admitted to hospital in Victoria for a condition that required an MRI scan. Her doctor told her not to travel to Canberra. Because Liberal Party rules stipulated that voting could only take place in person, Bailey did not vote. Without her support, Malcolm Turnbull lost, 41 votes to 42.[6] Afterwards, Bailey reported that a doctor had said the test results were 'thankfully clear'.[7]

Without Godwin Grech's fabrication, Andrew Robb's skulduggery, Joe Hockey's tweet, Tony Abbott's last-minute change of mind, and Fran Bailey's health scare, it is unlikely Malcolm Turnbull would have lost the Liberal leadership to Tony Abbott. Change any one of these five things and Abbott would most likely not have become leader in 2009, which makes it unlikely he would have become prime minister in 2013.

Australian leaders change remarkably frequently. Figure 4 estimates turnover among leaders and opposition leaders at the national, state and territory level since 1901.[8] Across leaders (the prime minister, premiers and chief ministers), an average of 25% get replaced every year. Among their opposition counterparts, 32% get replaced every year. Combined, the average

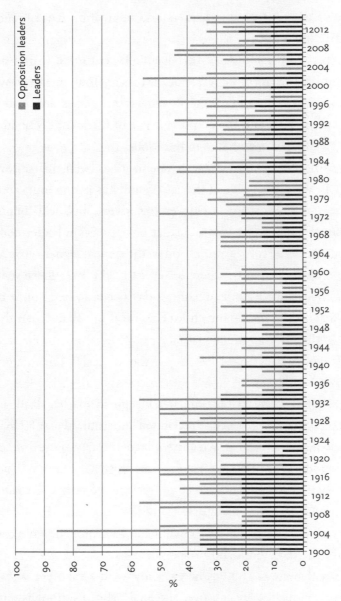

Figure 4: Annual turnover among leaders and opposition leaders

Leaders are premiers, chief ministers and the prime minister. Opposition leaders are their counterparts. 100% means that all leaders and opposition leaders change in a given year.

rate of turnover among leaders and opposition leaders since Federation is 29%.

In the first decade of the twentieth century, as our party structure was forming, it's not surprising that turnover was high (1904 saw nearly 90% of leaders and opposition leaders lose their jobs). But the combined rate of turnover declined to 20% in the 1950s and 16% in the 1960s.

Over the past four decades, turnover has been rising. It was 25% in the 1970s, 27% in the 1980s, and has been around 30% since the 1990s. More turnover means less political longevity. In the 1960s, the typical leader or opposition leader could expect to serve for six years. Today, the typical leader or opposition leader can only expect to serve for a bit over three years. The effect of luck on leadership today needs to be seen in the context of leaders having shorter political life spans than they did in the 1960s.

◆

On 7 April 1939, Prime Minister Joseph Lyons fell dead of a heart attack. His party, the United Australia Party (UAP), immediately set about selecting a leader. Party powerbrokers were keen to lure back former prime minister Stanley Bruce, but they were unable to do so on reasonable terms. Treasurer Richard Casey was a natural candidate, but lacked sufficient support in the party room. Finally, the vote came down to two people: Billy Hughes and Robert Menzies.

By that time, Hughes had already been a member of four other political parties (Labor, National Labor, Nationalist, and Australian). He was seventy-six years old, frail and severely deaf. But he worked hard to persuade UAP members to support him – placing supporters at the exits of Lyons' funeral service to lobby on his behalf, and promising the defence ministry to at least three different men.[9] It is a measure of the doubts that the UAP had about Menzies that he only defeated Hughes by four votes: 23 to 19.[10]

Although Menzies' first prime ministership lasted only two years, he stayed on as opposition leader, and went on to serve another sixteen years in the top job, becoming Australia's longest-serving prime minister. Many Liberal Party members still revere Menzies, praising his 'Forgotten People' speech and fondness for tradition. And yet if just two members of the UAP had switched their vote in 1939, Menzies may never have become prime minister.

Indeed, the 1939 vote is not the only lucky factor that led to Menzies becoming Australia's longest-serving prime minister. According to historian David Day, Menzies's four months in London in early 1941 led to a proposal by Churchill's opponents for Menzies to replace Churchill as British leader for the duration of the war.[11] The plan was reportedly backed by Viscount Astor, Lord Beaverbrook, war cabinet member Maurice Hankey and former British prime minister David Lloyd George. If the theory is true – and some historians dispute it – then the takeover would necessarily have required Menzies to resign his seat in the Australian parliament.[12]

For those parliamentarians who served in battle, the chances of war came to shape Australian politics.[13] In 1918, in the French region of Péronne, William Currey's company was being fired on by a 77-mm field gun from close range. Currey ran across open ground under machine-gun fire, killed the German crew and captured the weapon. The odds of his survival must surely have been low. His luck not only saw him win a Victoria Cross, but also live to enter the New South Wales parliament, where he served as a Labor member for seven years. On the other side of politics, Stanley Bruce was hit in the arm at Gallipoli, by a shot that could have been fatal if it had struck his chest instead. As it turned out, the wound spared him from joining a major operation by his battalion, which took the lives of many in his unit. Stanley Bruce went on to become Australia's eighth prime minister.

Some parliamentarians enlisted after being elected. New South Wales parliamentarian Ambrose Carmichael was twice wounded in France, yet survived to return to public life. Federal MP Granville Ryrie was twice wounded in Gallipoli, and participated in the Light Horse action that led to the capture of the town of Beersheba. Ryrie continued to serve in federal parliament until 1927. Not so fortunate was George Braund, who served in Gallipoli while a member of the New South Wales parliament. Returning from the frontlines, he took a shortcut through the scrub. He did not hear the challenge from an Australian sentry, and was shot dead.

The ultimate tragedy to affect a child is the loss of a parent. Yet there is evidence from the United Kingdom that childhood suffering and leadership go together. Seventeen of the past thirty-seven British prime ministers have lost a parent in childhood: a rate three times higher than in the general population.[14] Psychologists suggest that this may have to do with the 'Phaethon complex', in which childhood bereavement leads a person to take great risks in order to prove his or her worth. Applying simple theories to matters as complex as parental loss and leadership is a fraught exercise, but the statistics are striking nonetheless.

Two of Australia's longest-serving premiers came to power as a result of the unexpected deaths of others. In 1953, Henry Bolte became Victorian opposition leader when Trevor Oldham died in a plane crash on the way to attend Queen Elizabeth II's coronation. Two years later, Labor split over the issue of communism, and Bolte won the election. He was Victorian premier for seventeen years.

In 1968, the heart attack of Queensland premier Jack Pizzey led to Joh Bjelke-Petersen becoming premier, a job he kept for the next twenty-one years. Bjelke-Petersen benefited from Queensland's 'gerrymander' – originally introduced by Labor – which gave more weight to rural seats. The gerrymander allowed Bjelke-Petersen's Country Party to dominate Queensland politics despite receiving fewer votes than either the Liberal or Labor parties. For example, the 1969 election saw Labor receive more votes than the Liberal and Country parties combined, but the electoral system gave Labor thirty-one seats and the Coalition parties forty-five. (Things were worse in South Australia, where the Liberals won the 1962 election despite Labor gaining 54% of the vote.)

In New South Wales, Bob Carr had entered state politics in 1983 with the notion of shifting to federal parliament, and perhaps one day becoming foreign minister. Then, after the 1988 election, he was pressed into becoming state Labor leader. Carr famously wrote: 'I spent today like a doomed man ... I feel a jolt in the stomach at what I'm getting myself in for. It will destroy my career in four years.'[15] Seven years later, Carr would begin a decade-long premiership, the longest unbroken spell of a New South Wales premier. Then in 2012, a further piece of luck – the simultaneous resignation of the foreign minister (Kevin Rudd) and one of the New South Wales senators (Mark Arbib) – saw Carr achieve his dream of being appointed Australian foreign minister.

In Western Australia, Colin Barnett was within two months of leaving state politics when revelations emerged of Liberal leader Troy Buswell engaging in bizarre antics, including sniffing the chair of a female staffer. When Buswell resigned, Barnett reversed his decision to retire and instead took his party's leadership. Barnett won the 2008 election, and at the time of writing is a long-serving premier of Western Australia. As the saying goes, the difference between salad and compost is timing.

Like Menzies, other Australian prime ministers have had significant luck in their careers. As I noted at the start of this chapter, Tony Abbott won the leadership of his party over Malcolm Turnbull in 2009 by just one vote. A single vote also saw the downfall of Liberal Party prime minister John Gorton. In 1971, the Liberal Party room voted on a motion of confidence in John Gorton's leadership. The ballot was tied, and Gorton took it upon himself to resign.

Eighteen months later, after the Coalition lost the 1972 election, the Liberals voted to select the opposition leader. The initial party room ballot saw Billy Snedden and Nigel Bowen tied, with one parliamentarian having failed to cast a vote. A fresh ballot induced that person to vote for Snedden, who won by a single vote. Snedden remained leader until the 1974 election. Describing the result of that election, Snedden famously said of his party: 'We were not defeated. We did not win enough seats to form a government.'[16] Shortly afterwards, he was challenged for the Liberal leadership by Malcolm Fraser.[17] Snedden did not win enough votes to keep his job.

A senior Labor figure of that era, Bill Hayden, argues that if Snedden had not pushed the Whitlam government to hold an early election in 1974, he would have remained Liberal Party leader and won the 1975 election.[18] The closer the race, the more often that idiosyncratic factors – such as Joe Hockey asking Twitter for advice on climate change policy – come to affect the result. In recent years, there has been a succession of tight Liberal leadership ballots. In 2007, Brendan Nelson beat Turnbull by three votes. In 2008, Turnbull beat Nelson by four votes.

In the Labor party room, a similar pattern holds. In 1966, Gough Whitlam described the ALP National Executive as '12 witless men'. The executive responded by convening a meeting to consider expelling him, as they had done to Jack Lang some decades earlier. Initially, the forces against Whitlam, supported by Labor leader Arthur Calwell, appeared to have the numbers. As biographer Jenny Hocking recounts: 'As Arthur Calwell casually sat reading Ranke's *The History of the Popes*, confident in the certainty of Whitlam's imminent expulsion, the Queensland delegates switched their votes and voted for him. Whitlam was saved from expulsion by the narrowest margin: 7 votes to 5.'[19]

Eleven years later, after leading Australia's most avant-garde government, Whitlam found himself contesting the opposition leadership against Bill Hayden. A vote in the Labor caucus before the 1977 election saw Whitlam beat Hayden by just two votes. After the election, Whitlam resigned, and Hayden won the leadership.

In 1982, Hayden in turn was challenged by Bob Hawke, and won by only five votes. The next year, Hayden resigned the leadership and Hawke was elected unopposed. When Paul Keating successfully challenged Bob Hawke in December 1991 for the Labor leadership (and therefore the prime minister-ship), Keating won by just five votes.

In December 2003, Labor opposition leader Simon Crean stepped down, and Mark Latham beat Kim Beazley for the leadership by two votes. Latham would not have come out on top in a three-way contest, and was only able to win because Crean – having seen off a challenge in June 2003 from Beazley – urged his supporters to back Latham.

Yet Crean's decision was not enough to deliver the leader-ship to Latham. On the evening before the ballot, with a tied vote looking a real possibility, Latham went to see New South Wales MP Robert McClelland. McClelland told him that he would be backing Beazley on the grounds of his experience. Latham suggested that McClelland seek the advice of rugby league player Robert Stone.[20] In the late 1970s and early 1980s, Stone played first grade for St George, the team that Latham and McClelland both supported.

The next morning – a few hours before the ballot – McClelland called the retired rugby league player. Stone was surprised to get the phone call, but offered unambiguous advice: 'It's got to be Latham. Putting Beazley back in again would be like putting me into a first-grade team again. I'd be massacred. You have to move on and try something different.'[21] After a shower and a coffee, McClelland switched his vote to Latham. Had he not done so, the winner would have been drawn from a hat. Less than two years later, Stone died of a brain tumour.

Table 6 shows the results of some of the ballots that have decided who would lead Australia's major political parties in recent generations. The list is not exhaustive (for example, it excludes the quixotic challengers who took on H.V. Evatt in 1954 and 1956), but it covers twenty-two major leadership contests. On average, the winner took 57% of the vote, and many of the contests – particularly in recent decades – were determined by even slimmer margins.

Table 6: Major Australian leadership ballots

YEAR	PARTY	POSITION	RESULT	WINNER'S VOTE SHARE (%)
CLOSE (WINNER GOT 50–54%)				
1971	Liberal	Prime minister	William McMahon 33 tied with John Gorton 33 (Gorton then resigned)	50
2009	Liberal	Opposition leader	Tony Abbott 42 beat Malcolm Turnbull 41	51
1972	Liberal	Opposition leader	Billy Snedden 30 beat Nigel Bowen 29	51
1977	Labor	Opposition leader	Gough Whitlam 32 beat Bill Hayden 30	52
2003	Labor	Opposition leader	Mark Latham 47 beat Kim Beazley 45	51
2007	Liberal	Opposition leader	Brendan Nelson 45 beat Malcolm Turnbull 42	52
2008	Liberal	Opposition leader	Malcolm Turnbull 45 beat Brendan Nelson 41	52
1991	Labor	Prime minister	Paul Keating 56 beat Bob Hawke 51	52
1982	Labor	Opposition leader	Bill Hayden 42 beat Bob Hawke 37	53
1994	Liberal	Opposition leader	Alexander Downer 43 beat John Hewson 36	54

cont.

YEAR	PARTY	POSITION	RESULT	WINNER'S VOTE SHARE (%)
CLEAR (WINNER GOT 55–59%)				
1939	UAP	Prime minister	Robert Menzies 23 beat Billy Hughes 19	55
2006	Labor	Opposition leader	Kevin Rudd 49 beat Kim Beazley 39	56
2013	Labor	Prime minister	Kevin Rudd 57 beat Julia Gillard 45	56
1967	Labor	Opposition leader	Gough Whitlam 39 beat Jim Cairns 15 and Frank Crean 14	57
1975	Liberal	Opposition leader	Malcolm Fraser 37 beat Billy Snedden 27	58
DECISIVE (WINNER GOT 60% OR BETTER)				
1991	Labor	Prime minister	Bob Hawke 66 beat Paul Keating 44	60
1989	Liberal	Opposition leader	Andrew Peacock 44 beat John Howard 27	62
2003	Labor	Opposition leader	Simon Crean 58 beat Kim Beazley 34	63
1966	Labor	Opposition leader	Arthur Calwell 49 beat Gough Whitlam 25	66
1981	Liberal	Prime minister	Malcolm Fraser 54 beat Andrew Peacock 27	67
DECISIVE (WINNER GOT 60% OR BETTER)				
1945	Labor	Prime minister	Ben Chifley 49 beat Frank Forde 15, Norman Makin 7 and H.V. Evatt 2	67
2012	Labor	Prime minister	Julia Gillard 71 beat Kevin Rudd 31	70

The leadership winds that buffet party room ballots aren't all whirligigs like Fran Bailey's health and Robert Stone's breakfast phone call. One systematic source of luck for leaders is the world economy. In the last chapter, we saw that political parties that govern when the world economy is booming are more likely to be re-elected than parties that govern in a global slump. This occurs because voters commit the 'fundamental attribution error', mistakenly booting out national governments when the world economy goes sour.

The fundamental attribution error is the tendency for humans to overplay the role of individuals and underplay the role of circumstances. On the sports field, it explains why we tend to think the same batsman is more talented when he is playing at the Adelaide Oval (with its classic even bounce) than on the Melbourne Cricket Ground (with its longer boundaries). Try as we might, our brains aren't very good at measuring performance relative to the size of the ground.

The fundamental attribution error is why sports commentators speak about players who are 'on a roll', when they're merely observing Lady Luck at work. In business, the fundamental attribution error explains why chief executives who govern during a boom tend to be overpaid. In a boom, company boards often fail to measure their CEO against the rest of the market. They forget that they are just surfing the wave like everyone else.

As humans, we're not very good at separating individual performance from the environment in which it happens. And it turns out that voters aren't the only ones who commit this error when selecting between parties. Party colleagues also make it when choosing a leader. As a result, the world economy also affects leaders' careers.

Analysing leadership turnover, Paul Burke finds that democratic leaders are more likely to lose their job when the economy goes sour.[22] This holds even when he looks at slumps caused by factors entirely outside the leader's control, such as drought (for farming countries) or low global commodity prices (for commodity-exporting nations). Drop global growth by 1 percentage point, and the chance of the ruling party in a democracy changing leader rises by 2.3 percentage points.

This result suggests that at the height of the global financial crisis, around eleven national leaders per year were prematurely removed from office. Around the world, party rooms may think that they are judging individual contenders purely on merit, but one of the best predictors of whether a party will replace its leader is the world growth rate.

When the early 1990s recession hit, it wasn't just the Australian Labor Party that removed a prime minister (Bob Hawke). During the same global slump, the UK Conservative Party ousted Prime Minister Margaret Thatcher, the Belgian Christian Democrats ousted Prime Minister Wilfried Martens, and the Irish Fianna Fáil party removed Prime Minister Charles Haughey.

After the 2001 election, journalists began to speculate about Peter Costello's ambitions to become prime minister. At one point, Costello himself fuelled rumours by replying that someone with his 'track record of loyalty'[23] shouldn't have to reply to questions of that kind. It was a cheeky response because it echoed Howard's answer when asked in 1984 whether he would challenge Andrew Peacock (Howard replaced Peacock as leader the year after making the comment).[24]

And yet strong global growth ultimately hampered Peter Costello's quest for the prime ministership. Even as many suggested that it was time for generational change, the booming world economy meant that the Liberal party room could not bring themselves to remove Howard as leader. Costello was treasurer in such good economic times that Paul Keating once said he had been 'hit in the arse by a rainbow'.[25] But in terms of promotion, Costello was also unlucky, since that same economic growth prevented him from ever becoming prime minister.

So it turns out that – like factory workers – political leaders are more likely to lose their jobs in a recession. But from an economic perspective, does it matter? Are national leaders a major influence on the economy, or doesn't it matter which jockey rides the horse?

One of the strongest proponents of the leadership-is-overrated school of thought was Leo Tolstoy, who argued that 'great men – so-called – are but labels serving to give a name to the event'.[26] Yet as a plethora of political biographies attests, the view that individuals matter remains powerful. Isn't it tempting to believe that individuals matter more than mere political parties and the nameless forces of history?

Perhaps the most tantalising version of the leadership-is-everything perspective is counterfactual history. If Harold Holt had not drowned at Cheviot Beach on 17 December 1967, would the Coalition have avoided the problems that beset his successors? If Neville Wran had not been handicapped by a throat operation in June 1980, would he have entered federal politics before Bob Hawke and been an even more successful leader?[27]

In an intriguing article, two US economists, Ben Jones and Ben Olken, set about assessing the impact of leadership on a nation's economic outcomes.[28] To ascertain the causal impact, they examined cases in which leaders die from accidents or natural causes. In effect, they asked: did the deaths of John Curtin, Gamal Abdel Nasser and Franklin D. Roosevelt change their nations' economic trajectories?

The answer is that Tolstoy was half-right. Leaders affect the economic growth rate in autocracies, but not in democracies. The deaths of Ayatollah Khomeini and Mao Zedong were followed by rapid improvements in living standards for ordinary Iranians and Chinese. But in a typical democracy, there is no immediate change in economic outcomes when a leader passes away. Constrained by political parties, institutions and interest groups, democratic leaders have less scope to make sudden changes in economic policy than the typical biography might have you think.

Admittedly, these results do not rule out any leader effects whatsoever. It could be that while most leaders are interchangeable with the other grey suits in their party, a handful stand out from the crowd. Or maybe leaders have little impact on short-run economic growth, but nonetheless leave their mark on foreign policy, income inequality, public infrastructure or the configuration of the public service. Such leadership might include Winston Churchill's stirring wartime radio broadcasts, Ronald Reagan's pressure on the Soviet Union, John Howard's gun buyback, or Kevin Rudd's apology to the Stolen Generations.

In autocracies, leaders matter not only for economic growth, but also for their nation's political system. The best proof of this comes from another study by Jones and Olken. This time they look not at natural deaths, but at assassinations versus near misses.[29]

As noted in Chapter 1, there is plenty of luck involved in whether an assassination succeeds or fails. In 1939, Hitler was visiting a Munich beer hall when his staff told him that bad weather had forced the cancellation of his return flight and that he would need to leave early to catch a train instead. The decision likely saved Hitler's life, as the assassin's bomb left for him exploded 13 minutes after his departure.

Table 7 shows examples of successful assassinations, such as the shootings of Sadat, Hee Park and Laurent Kabila. These are compared with unsuccessful assassinations, such as the 1976 attempt on the life of Ugandan dictator Idi Amin, which saw a grenade bounce off his chest and into the nearby crowd, killing several bystanders.[30] Jones and Olken find that successful assassinations raise the odds of a transition from autocracy to democracy by 13 percentage points. Near misses have no impact.

Table 7: Assassinations and attempted assassinations in autocracies

ASSASSINATIONS	NEAR MISSES
Boris III (Bulgaria, 1943)	Lon Nol (Cambodia, 1973)
Laurent Kabila (Congo Kinshasa, 2001)	Pinochet (Chile, 1986)
Sadat (Egypt, 1981)	Mao Zedong (China, 1961)
Hee Park (South Korea, 1979)	Hitler (Germany, 1939 and 1944)
Alexander II (Russia, 1881)	Sukarno (Indonesia, 1957 and 1962)
Habyarimana (Rwanda, 1994)	Saddam Hussein (Iraq, 1982)
Faisal (Saudi Arabia, 1975)	Mussolini (Italy, 1923, 1924, 1926)
Delgado Chalbaud (Venezuela, 1950)	Idi Amin (Uganda, 1975 and 1976)
Transitions to democracy in following year: 13 percentage points higher	Transitions to democracy in following year: No difference

Source: Ben Jones and Ben Olken, 2009, 'Hit or miss? The effect of assassinations on institutions and war'

After the death of Abraham Lincoln, Benjamin Disraeli opined that 'assassination has never changed the history of the world'. When it comes to autocracies, Disraeli was wrong. The data show that the same events that spell bad luck for dictators are good luck for democratisers.

♠

Now, let's ask the question in reverse: is it true that the fate of individual politicians influences the economy? My analysis focuses on a particular measure of business confidence: the share market. Share prices are only one economic statistic, but they do have the advantage that they're available at high frequency. Moreover, the standard economic view is that share prices incorporate all publicly available information. So if an unexpected event happens, the change in share prices reflects the market's view on how much that event is likely to affect the earnings of publicly traded companies.

Table 8 shows the share market response to the fourteen leadership transitions in Australian politics from 1945 to 2013.[31] Overall, what is striking is how small the effects are, relative to typical day-to-day movements in the stock market. In a typical week, there is a day on which the share market falls by 0.6%, and another day when it rises by a similar amount. In a typical month, there is a day when the share market falls by 1.4%, and a day when it rises by just as much. And in the typical year, there is a day when the market falls by 3.5%, and a day when it rises by about as much.[32]

How much can the share market move in a single day? As luck would have it, the three largest one-day falls in the past three decades have each taken place in October. On 20 October 1987 ('Black Tuesday'), the share market dropped 25%. On 16 October 1989 (in response to problems in the US junk bond market), the Australian share market dropped 8%. And the market also dropped 8% on 10 October 2008 ('Black Friday'), in response to the global financial crisis. Moving from bears to bulls, the market rose by 6% on 28 October 1987, 13 November 1987, 29 October 1997 and 25 November 2008.

On this scale, changes in the prime minister have a negligible impact on the Australian share market. The three most unexpected changes were the 1967 drowning of Harold Holt (associated with a 0.1% increase in the market), the 1971 change from John Gorton to William McMahon (associated with a 1.6% rise in the market) and the 2010 change from Kevin Rudd to Julia Gillard (associated with a 0.1% fall in the market). The 1967 and 2010 share market movements are trivial, and the 1971 rise is of the size that typically occurs once every month or so.

Even the largest share price movements in Table 8 (overleaf) are dwarfed by the impact of financial events. Moreover, there is no strong partisan pattern. On average, transitions from Labor to Liberal prime ministers see the stock market rise 0.3%, while transitions from Liberal to Labor prime ministers see the stock market rise 0.8%. Changes from one Liberal prime minister to another are associated with a 0.5% rise, while changes from one Labor prime minister to another are associated with a 0.3% rise. Prime ministerial changes – whether expected or unexpected, to the same party or a different party – have little impact on share prices. This implies that investors see the prime minister as having a minimal effect on the profitability of the typical firm.[33]

♣

Table 8: How much do prime ministers affect the share market?

OUTGOING PM	SUCCESSOR	EVENT	DATE	EXPECTED?	IMPACT (%)
John Curtin	Uncertain	Death	5 July 1945	Somewhat expected	None
Ben Chifley	Robert Menzies	Election	10 December 1949	Somewhat expected	+0.5
Robert Menzies	Harold Holt	Resignation	20 January 1966	Reasonably expected	−0.1
Harold Holt	Uncertain	Death	17 December 1967	Entirely unexpected	+0.1
John Gorton	William McMahon	Party room ballot	10 March 1971	Quite unexpected	+1.6
William McMahon	Gough Whitlam	Election	2 December 1972	Reasonably expected	None
Gough Whitlam	Malcolm Fraser	Election	13 December 1975	Somewhat expected	−0.1
Malcolm Fraser	Bob Hawke	Election	5 March 1983	Reasonably expected	+0.2
Bob Hawke	Paul Keating	Party room ballot	19 December 1991	Reasonably expected	−0.5
Paul Keating	John Howard	Election	2 March 1996	Reasonably expected	+0.2
John Howard	Kevin Rudd	Election	24 November 2007	Reasonably expected	+2.2
Kevin Rudd	Julia Gillard	Party room ballot	24 June 2010	Quite unexpected	−0.1
Julia Gillard	Kevin Rudd	Party room ballot	26 June 2013	Somewhat expected	+1.6
Kevin Rudd	Tony Abbott	Election	7 September 2013	Reasonably expected	+0.7

In politics, as in sprinting and clay pigeon shooting, timing can be critical. Melbournians Peter Costello and Lindsay Tanner were both regarded as shining lights of their respective parties when they entered parliament in the early 1990s. Both rose quickly within their parties, and served for around two decades (Costello from 1990 to 2009, Tanner from 1993 to 2010). Yet by the time they retired, Costello had spent eleven years as a minister, and Tanner just three.

In terms of ministerial careers, there are few luckier surfers of the political waves than Peter Costello, and few unluckier than Lindsay Tanner. Had Australia followed a different political cycle, their fortunes would have been reversed. For example, British Labour held office from 1997 to 2010. If this cycle had been followed in Australia, it's likely that Tanner would have served as a minister for thirteen years rather than three.

But don't feel as sorry for Lindsay Tanner as for Charles Griffiths, who entered federal politics at age forty-six as the Labor member for Shortland (in the New South Wales Hunter region). Griffiths retired at age sixty-nine, following an unusually long parliamentary career of twenty-three years. Alas, his service perfectly coincided with federal Labor's longest stint out of power: 1949 to 1972. In more than two decades in federal parliament, Griffiths never once sat on the government side of the House of Representatives.

When he took on the job of Leader of the House in 1972, Fred Daly's first action was to move 'that the question be put,' remarking triumphantly, 'I've waited almost thirty years to do that.'[34] Daly was one of only three members of the Whitlam government with experience of government.

While spending your entire career in opposition is less than ideal, it doesn't follow that opposition is always bad for a person's career. Indeed, if you want the top job, the ideal time to enter parliament is when your party is in opposition. In opposition, there are fewer people in your party room to compete with (if there were more, your party would be in government), and more opportunities to raise your profile by running campaigns on particular issues.

Most MPs enter parliament at a time when their party is in power. By contrast, the last six people to become prime minister – Tony Abbott, Kevin Rudd, Julia Gillard, John Howard, Paul Keating and Bob Hawke – started their careers when their party was in opposition. They got their first front-bench job quickly, did it well, and garnered rapid promotion.[35]

For becoming a cabinet minister, timing of entry into politics matters, but in a different sense. An analysis by Michael Dalvean finds a striking regularity in the promotion patterns of Coalition and Labor parliamentarians. On average, promotion to cabinet is more likely for those who enter politics at a younger age.[36] The average age of entry into parliament is thirty-eight for those who end up as cabinet ministers, compared with forty-three for those who do not end up as cabinet ministers. Since most people take the first available chance to enter parliament, the age of entry is largely random – determined by a retirement or a national election swing. So the luck of getting elected at a younger age translates to a more senior career.

With a fixed number of positions on the front bench, every promotion requires someone more senior to retire – either voluntarily or involuntarily. Just as the twelfth man in cricket only takes the field when one of the first eleven are injured, so too a gap must emerge in the senior ranks for a politician to be promoted.

Paul Keating's ascension to treasurer is a perfect example of this. In January 1983, Labor leader Bill Hayden decided to remove Shadow Treasurer Ralph Willis, and replace him with Keating. The following month, Bob Hawke won the Labor leadership, and became prime minister in March.

Hawke was personally close to Willis, and was at first quite confident that after the election he could reinstate him as treasurer and give Keating some other portfolio.[37] As Keating recalls, he said to Hawke that if there was any attempt to remove him, 'I'll invoke the Harry Truman doctrine of massive retaliation.'[38] Given Keating's senior status in the New South Wales Right faction, Hawke retained him as treasurer, and Keating served in that role for the next eight years. Keating was possibly Australia's greatest ever treasurer, but had it not been for his luck in Hayden demoting Willis, he might never have served in the job.

◆

As the far-right British politician Enoch Powell noted, 'All political lives, unless they are cut off in midstream at a happy juncture, end in failure, because that is the nature of politics and of human affairs.' Since Federation, Australia has had twenty-eight prime ministers. Only six have left the job voluntarily – the most recent being Robert Menzies in 1966, nearly half a century ago. Just as luck plays a role in leaders rising to the top, so too has luck shaped many an undoing.

In 1974, the Whitlam government hatched a plan to improve its numbers in the Senate. Senator Vince Gair, of the minority Democratic Labor Party, had become disgruntled with his party, and was considering what he might do after politics. The government offered to appoint him as ambassador to Ireland, his mother's country of birth, and Gair happily accepted.

Yet for the plan to work, Gair had to formally tender his resignation before conservative Queensland premier Joh Bjelke-Petersen had issued the writs for the half-Senate election. To prevent this, two Nationals senators – Ian Wood and Ron Maunsell – devised a plan to keep Gair busy drinking beer and scotch, and eating the fresh prawns Maunsell had brought down from Townsville. The plan was a success: Gair failed to resign before the deadline, and the event became known as 'the Night of the Long Prawns'.[39]

The plot helped force Whitlam to call a full Senate election. In effect, a plan cleverly hatched by Labor was brought undone by the cunning of the Queensland Nationals. But it required some luck too: if Whitlam had realised what was occurring, he would have ensured Gair resigned. And if Gair hadn't been in the mood for socialising, hadn't liked prawns or had been a little less inebriated, the course of Australian history might have been changed.

Yet an even greater piece of bad luck was to hit the Whitlam government the next year, in the form of a heart attack. Heart attacks arise from a build-up of plaque around the walls of coronary arteries. The build-up itself isn't luck: you can significantly reduce your risk of a heart attack by eating well and exercising regularly. But the timing of the heart attack itself is effectively a matter of luck. The plaque builds up over decades, and then within minutes cascades into the artery, sometimes blocking it entirely.

Heart attacks can be triggered by a stressful event, or they can come about entirely unexpectedly. There's luck in who is around when the heart attack happens. Both my grandfathers – Keith Leigh and Roly Stebbins – experienced heart attacks that stopped their hearts. Keith was out running on his own, while Roly was with his wife. Keith died, but quick action by the paramedics gave Roly another quarter century of life.

In the case of Labor senator Bertie Milliner, his heart attack came at age sixty-three, when he was in his Brisbane office.[40] The tragedy of Milliner's death was exploited by the Queensland National Party. Breaking with convention, Bjelke-Petersen refused to nominate Labor's preferred candidate as the replacement. Instead, Bjelke-Petersen opted for a disgruntled member of the Labor Party. This followed a similar decision earlier that year, when the New South Wales premier had appointed a non-Labor senator to replace retiring Labor senator Lionel Murphy. It meant the numbers in the Senate were effectively 30 Coalition and 29 Labor, which allowed the Coalition to block supply.[41]

The final piece of bad luck came in the form of Governor-General John Kerr. When choosing a new governor-general in 1974, Gough Whitlam had first approached businessman and philanthropist Kenneth Myer.[42] Myer turned down the job, perhaps because his wife was Japanese and he was worried about ill-feeling from World War II veterans. Whitlam then approached Treasurer Frank Crean, who said 'Not yet' (Crean might have felt otherwise if he had known that his time as treasurer had only a year left to run). Kerr was Whitlam's third choice as governor-general.

At the heart of the 1975 Dismissal was an interpretation of the constitutional 'reserve powers'. Whitlam's view was that the governor-general had no personal discretion to act against the prime minister – that reserve powers did not exist. Kerr, by contrast, had been thinking about the reserve powers since the age of seventeen, when Labor's H.V. Evatt persuaded him that the governor-general did indeed have such a capacity.

As Paul Kelly notes, 'Out of virtually all the candidates Whitlam could have chosen as Governor-General, he picked a man who by personal experience and intellectual belief was most likely to accept the existence of reserve powers, and most likely to reject any proposition put to him as Governor-General that attempted to deny their existence.'[43] Faced with a situation in which supply had been blocked, Kerr dismissed the government. Had either Kenneth Myer or Frank Crean accepted the position of governor-general, the Dismissal would probably not have happened.

A heart attack also helped hasten the end of the Hawke government. On 7 December 1990, Treasurer Paul Keating was scheduled to give an off-the-record speech to the parliamentary press gallery.[44] The previous night, his 47-year-old treasury secretary, Chris Higgins, had died suddenly of a heart attack after competing in a Canberra athletics meeting. The tragedy led Keating to deliver a sharper, more melancholy speech. He began by saying that 'this game is all about whether you want to be a participant or a voyeur. Chris Higgins was a participant and a participant by choice, and that choice remains open to all of us in public life, and in journalism.'[45] Then Keating went on to reflect that the United States had had three great leaders – Washington, Lincoln and Roosevelt – and yet Australia had not had a single one. He called John Curtin a 'trier'.

Keating contrasted his own style of leadership – 'trying to stream the economics and the politics together. Out there on the stage doing the Plácido Domingo' – with that of Prime Minister Bob Hawke – '[going] through some shopping centre, tripping over the TV crews' cords'. The speech infuriated Hawke – who claimed to be most outraged by the critique of Curtin rather than himself. It led to Hawke breaking the 'Kirribilli Agreement' to hand over the prime ministership to Keating, and to Keating challenging Hawke for the leadership in June 1991. If Chris Higgins had not died, it is possible that Keating would have been more circumspect, and that the Hawke–Keating rivalry would have remained out of the public eye for somewhat longer.[46]

For the most part, I've focused in this chapter on the luck of getting to the top. But successful leadership isn't just about occupying a senior job – it's also a matter of what you achieve in it. Part of this depends on certain valuable traits: the ability to work hard, inspire loyalty and communicate effectively. But other characteristics aren't so clear-cut. Remember Thomas Nagel's notion of circumstantial luck? The idea that life is about the interplay between your personal traits and the circumstances around you applies to leaders too. The personal attributes that make for success in one setting might cause a leader to fail in a different one.

Discussing mental illness and leadership, Nassir Ghaemi contrasts the US Civil War generals George McClellan and William Sherman.[47] In peacetime, he argues, McClellan might have been regarded as a precocious sensation. But when put to the test in a new battle environment, he proved a dud. Sherman, by contrast, created the notion of 'total war' – the destruction of the productive capacity of the south. Faced with a new challenge, Sherman's 'insane genius' helped the north win the Civil War.

In politics, Ghaemi contrasts Neville Chamberlain, who he says was perfect in peacetime but horrendous as war loomed, with Winston Churchill, 'terrible in peace, sublime in war'.[48]

He quotes Churchill's 1940 eulogy for Chamberlain: 'In one phase men might seem to have been right: in another they seem to have been wrong, and when the perspective of time lengthened, all stood in a different setting.'[49]

Churchill was right to lead his nation in World War II. Without that terrible conflict, his would have been a very different career. As biographer Robert James notes, 'If the story had ended in 1938 or even 1939, we should be in the presence of a great personal tragedy. We should be obliged to dwell upon the moral that great abilities and industry cannot, in themselves, secure political success. We should have pondered on the paradox that a mind so fertile and a character so many-faceted should have proved incapable.'[50]

Australian politics is full of examples of leaders whose traits were right or wrong for the times. Billy Hughes' divisive leadership in World War I (he called opponents of conscription 'traitors') was bad for Australia, and his excessive demands on Germany contributed to the punitive settlement that helped lay the groundwork for World War II.[51] By contrast, John Curtin was willing to stand up to Churchill on the question of Australian troops returning home, and to call on America for support.

Gough Whitlam's government had the right social policies to bring Australia out of the 1960s, but its economic policies were inadequate in the face of the stagflation of the 1970s. When the Port Arthur tragedy happened, John Howard's willingness to lead on gun control led to a National Firearms Agreement that a Labor prime minister probably could not have achieved. Asked to name the biggest challenge for a political leader, British prime minister Harold Macmillan is said to have replied, 'Events, dear boy, events.'[52]

Events affect not only political careers, but also the outcome of issues. What gets buried and what receives prominence? When can oppositions scare governments into adopting their policies? Can luck affect policies on major issues – even, say, as big as climate change?

7

CLIMATE, BABY BONUS AND RECESSION – HOW LUCK AFFECTS WHAT GOVERNMENT DOES

In late 2006, many parts of eastern Australia were in the grip of a multi-year drought. Most people lived under severe water restrictions. The bushfire season started early. Prime Minister John Howard described the situation as a 'perfect storm'. He had to be seen as 'doing something' on climate change, so Howard decided to give a major address to the Melbourne Press Club. In that address, given a few months before the election, Howard described the science on climate change as 'compelling' and committed his government to implement an emissions trading scheme.[1]

In 2013, Howard admitted that his decision to act on climate change was based purely on politics, saying that he had 'always been something of an agnostic on global warming'.[2] And the politics, he noted, were partly driven by the weather. In 2006, Australia received half its average annual rainfall, and experienced the highest average temperatures since the 1950s. In that year, 68% of Australians agreed with the statement 'Global warming is a serious and pressing problem'. By 2010, after the drought had eased, just 46% held that view. In 2013, it was 40%.[3]

The link between current weather patterns and attitudes to climate change has been confirmed by researchers from Columbia University.[4] On days when the temperature is warmer than usual, respondents are more likely to believe that climate change is occurring, and more likely to be personally worried about it. The study authors liken their findings to a classic science experiment: if you hold an ice cube in your left hand and a hot drink in your right hand, then put both hands into room temperature water, the water will feel warm (to your left hand) but cold (to your right hand).[5] Perspective matters.

The breaking of the drought was a welcome relief to Australia's farmers, and the relaxation of household water restrictions was a boon to gardeners. But the political effect of these climatic changes was to take the pressure off those who favoured strong action. In 2009, when Abbott replaced Turnbull as Liberal leader, the bipartisan consensus over climate change broke down.

Even then, the 2009 emissions trading scheme package teetered on the brink. Two Liberal senators – Judith Troeth and Sue Boyce – crossed the floor, which meant that the package needed only the support of the Greens to become law. Two years later, the Greens would support a very similar package.[6] But in 2009, they opted to vote against emissions trading and the Senate vote was lost.

Because this is a book about luck and politics, previous chapters have largely focused on individuals, parties and governments. By now, I hope I've persuaded you that luck affects the careers of particular politicians, and shapes whether a government stands or falls.

But you might still ask: so what? Who cares if a few wannabe politicians miss out as a result of luck, or even if the occasional government falls because of factors outside its control? Cricket, rugby and tennis are replete with instances of how players and teams are affected by luck, but chance on the sporting field doesn't change Australia. Couldn't it be the case that luck affects the sport of politics, but not the fabric of society?

This chapter aims to answer these questions by moving beyond politicians and parties to look at outcomes. How has luck shaped the world we live in?

In 1993, Israeli prime minister Yitzhak Rabin stood on the South Lawn of the White House and reluctantly extended his hand to Palestine Liberation Organization leader Yasir Arafat. 'The time for peace has come,' Rabin declared. 'We who have fought against you, the Palestinians – we say today in a loud and clear voice: enough of blood and tears. Enough.'[7]

Among mainstream Israelis, Rabin carried the credibility of having been the chief of his nation's armed forces in 1967, when Israel carried out a preventive strike against neighbours who were threatening to attack. His handshake with Arafat led to a Nobel Peace Prize the following year. In 1995, he signed the Oslo Accords, and began to withdraw Israeli forces from the West Bank. Peace, it seemed, was within reach.

But Rabin infuriated Israel's ultranationalists, who saw him betraying the biblical destiny of the Jewish people. At a rally in Tel Aviv, a right-wing law student named Yigal Amir walked up to Rabin and fired three shots with a Beretta pistol. Rabin died in hospital from his wounds.

As with other assassinations, there was an element of chance. Rabin might have survived if his bodyguards had reacted faster, or if all three bullets had missed him (only one did). The tragedy might also have been averted if Israel's internal security agency Shin Bet had heeded the threat that Amir posed to Rabin.

Two decades after Rabin's death, his brand of moderate politics is considerably weaker. In 2015, Israeli prime minister Benjamin Netanyahu won re-election by telling voters that there would be no independent Palestinian state while he was in charge.[8] That stance, along with changes in the Palestinian leadership, make the prospects of peace seem more remote than they did in 1995. Palestinian extremists fire rockets at Israeli towns on a weekly basis. Israel's 2014 intervention in Gaza cost over 2000 lives. It is difficult to avoid the conclusion that the killing of Yitzhak Rabin set back the Israeli–Palestinian peace process by at least a generation.

Six years after losing the 2000 US presidential election, Al Gore gave a mock presidential address on the television show *Saturday Night Live*, in which he gravely took 'responsibility' for saving social security, stopping global warming, bringing down petrol prices to 5 cents a litre, and keeping the US out of conflict in the Middle East.

The 2000 election was one of the closest in US history. Nationwide, Gore had half a million more votes than Bush, but the result came down to Florida. On the night of the election, the television networks called Florida for Gore at 8 pm, then for Bush at 2 am. By daybreak, it was evident that the election would be too close to call. Of the six million votes cast in Florida, the gap between the two candidates was just a few hundred.

This prompted a mandatory recount, and attention began to focus on the oddities of Florida's voting systems. Voters in Palm Beach were given 'butterfly ballots', in which candidates were listed in two columns, but the punch holes were in a single line down the centre. As right-wing presidential candidate Pat Buchanan admitted, when he looked at the ballot, he could readily see how some Gore supporters might have accidentally voted for him on the butterfly ballot.

Another issue arose where punch machines had not fully removed the small circle of paper, or 'chad'. If the chad was 'hanging', 'dimpled' or 'pregnant', should it count as a vote? Florida's counties applied conflicting standards, and a subsequent study concluded that applying a consistent rule statewide would have seen Gore win by between 60 and 171 votes.[9]

When the recount in two key counties had not been completed by the deadline, the Florida Supreme Court ordered a recount of votes that had been rejected by machine counters. A fortnight later, by a one-vote margin, the US Supreme Court ordered that the previous official count should stand. Bush was declared the winner of Florida, and therefore the presidency. As Gore later noted, 'you win some, you lose some. And then there's that little-known third category'.[10] Four years later, Bush won re-election with the narrowest margin ever for an incumbent president.

Given the tightness of the 2000 and 2004 elections, not much would have had to change for the US to have Al Gore rather than George W. Bush as president from 2001 to 2009. Gore would surely not have pursued Bush's tax cuts, and would almost certainly have done more to combat climate change. After the September 11 terrorist attacks, it's likely that Gore would have responded with more sophistication (it's hard to imagine Gore offending millions of Muslims by talking about a US 'crusade', as Bush did on the eve of the 2003 war in Iraq).

Australia has had its own share of close races. In 1961, Robert Menzies' Coalition government squeaked home: sixty-two seats to sixty. The last seat decided was Moreton, won by the Liberal Party's Jim Killen with just 110 votes more than Labor. Ironically, Killen managed to win because he got just enough Communist Party preferences. Without Communist preferences going to the Liberal Party, Labor's Arthur Calwell would have become prime minister in 1961.

In the 1963 election, Labor was again performing well, when just eight days before polling day, US president John F. Kennedy was assassinated. Australians were transfixed by events in the United States, including the subsequent murder of Lee Harvey Oswald and Kennedy's funeral. As John Howard admits in his biography of Menzies, the assassination 'must have resulted in some undecided voters resolving to stay with the status quo at a time of international trauma'.[11] In case swing voters were unsure what lesson to draw from the events in Dallas, Menzies went so far as to use the late President Kennedy's name in a Liberal Party advertisement. Like Howard in 2001, Menzies in 1963 benefited electorally from a shocking international event close to polling day.

Had Labor won in 1961 or 1963, Prime Minister Calwell would have banned 'women's rates' of pay and expanded the stock of public housing.[12] He would have increased the number of Commonwealth scholarships for low-income students to attend university. A Calwell government would have boosted welfare payments such as age pensions, child endowment and maternity allowances. It is possible that Calwell might also have diversified Australia's trade in Asia (anticipating Britain's entry into the European common market) and limited Australia's involvement in the Vietnam War. The Calwell government might have accelerated economic development in northern Australia, and created a Medicare-style national health insurance scheme. Australia under Calwell in the 1960s would unquestionably have been changed. Indeed, it is unlikely that Australia today would be the same nation had either of those elections turned out differently.

Another form of electoral fortune is where the votes fall. To win an Australian election requires a majority of seats, not a majority of overall votes. In most cases, the party that garners the most votes also wins the most seats, but not always. Of the twenty-six Australian elections held in the post-war era, there have been five in which the losing party had a majority of the nationwide two-party vote. In 1954, Labor won 50.7%; in 1961, Labor won 50.5%; in 1969, Labor won 50.2%; in 1990, the Coalition won 50.1%; in 1998, Labor won 51.0%.[13] In each case, the party with more votes lost the election because too much of its support came in its safest seats, and too little in marginal seats. In every case, Australia would be a different nation today if the majority party had won the election. Not only would we have had prime ministers Evatt, Calwell, Peacock and Beazley, but the set of policies the government adopted would have taken Australia along a different path.

In 2010, commentator Peter Brent pointed out that just because we don't know which party will win an election, it doesn't follow that we should expect a hung parliament.[14] He likened it to AFL, where uncertainty about the result shouldn't lead fans to expect a draw. It was a fair point, but Brent's timing was unfortunate. That year, the AFL grand final between Collingwood and St Kilda was a draw. And for the first time in almost seventy years, 2010 saw the Australian people elect a hung parliament. Labor had seventy-two seats, the Coalition seventy-three, and Greens and independents held the remaining five seats. With the Coalition having more seats, some commentators expected them to form government. Other options were floated, such as independent Rob Oakeshott's proposal of a 'mix and match' government, with cabinet comprising senior figures from both parties.

After seventeen days of negotiations, a sufficient number of independents decided to support Labor. Had the independents decided differently, the Coalition would have formed government in 2010. In such an environment, Australia would not have enacted the National Disability Insurance Scheme, plain packaging of cigarettes or an emissions trading scheme. It is unlikely that the government would have sought a seat on the United Nations Security Council, and probable that it would have chosen a different mix of tax and welfare laws.

Prime Minister Gillard's negotiating skills clearly played an important part in Labor's win in 2010, but luck mattered too. Five house seats were decided by a margin of less than 1 percentage point – races so tight that idiosyncratic factors such as ballot order, weather and candidate names could easily have played a part in the outcome. Had the result in a couple of Labor's seats gone the other way, Abbott would have won. Had Labor picked up a few more seats, Gillard would have governed with an outright majority.

Luck not only shaped Labor's win in 2010, but also each of the bills passed by the forty-third parliament. The independents included three former National Party MPs, Tony Windsor, Rob Oakeshott and Bob Katter, and a former Liberal Party MP, Peter Slipper. Katter and Slipper mostly voted with the opposition, yet by the end of the parliament, nine bills had passed by a majority of one vote with Katter's support, including changes to fuel taxation, industrial relations and migration.[15] An opposition amendment to a health bill had been defeated by one vote (with Slipper voting with the government).[16] On a handful of occasions, the vote was tied, and the speaker's casting vote went with the government.[17]

In the period 2010 to 2013, almost all of the minor party and independent members in the House of Representatives proved decisive on particular policy issues. For the Gillard government, lining up the right constellation of supporters in the house was like threading a series of moving needles. No government bills were defeated, but several were withdrawn when it became clear that they would not pass the House, including bills on offshore processing of asylum seekers and media diversity. A bill on gambling law reform was never voted on because while it was championed by one independent (Andrew Wilkie), it was opposed by two others (Rob Oakeshott and Tony Windsor). Every new law shapes the country, and almost every bill passed by the forty-third parliament did so because of a combination of negotiating skills and luck.

In February 2004, three months after beating Kim Beazley for the opposition leadership by two votes, Mark Latham announced that Labor would support closing the superannuation schemes for parliamentarians, judges and the governor-general. The schemes, he argued, were 'well outside the community standard in Australia and have become out-of-date.'[18]

The immediate response to Latham's announcement by Howard government ministers Tony Abbott and Peter Costello was to defend the existing superannuation schemes. But two days after Latham committed Labor to closing the schemes to new entrants, Howard announced that the government would pass legislation to do just that.

Two months later, Latham again committed the Labor Party to a popular policy. The opposition, he announced, would take an expanded Baby Bonus policy to the election, with parents of a newborn baby receiving $3000 from the government.[19] The next month, Peter Costello brought down his ninth budget. A centrepiece of the budget was an expanded $3000 Baby Bonus. By the time it was scrapped in 2014, the Baby Bonus paid out over a billion dollars per year.

A year later, Latham was out of federal politics altogether. But the policy positions he adopted in opposition had a lasting effect. Had Robert McClelland not switched his vote in the December 2003 ballot, it's perfectly possible that Australia would have maintained its generous parliamentary superannuation schemes and not created a Baby Bonus.

On 29 November 1990, Treasurer Paul Keating faced the media to deliver more bad news. Since the start of the year, 160,000 people had joined the unemployment queue. Business confidence was in the doldrums. And now the Australian Bureau of Statistics had released estimates of the national accounts.

The national accounts have a particular importance in

Australia because of how our recessions are defined. In the United States, the timing of recessions is decided by a committee of experts from the National Bureau of Economic Research (with the alluring name of the 'Business Cycle Dating Committee'). But in Australia, the most common definition of a recession is when the size of the economy shrinks in two consecutive quarters.

Keating's media conference marked the release of the national accounts from the September quarter. According to the statistician, the economy had contracted for the second quarter in a row. Keating called it 'a recession that Australia had to have' – a line that would haunt him in years to come.

Yet the first release data were wrong. Over time, the Australian Bureau of Statistics has regularly revised its estimates of the September 1990 national accounts, using new data sources and more accurate modelling procedures. As commentator George Megalogenis has pointed out, their best contemporary estimate is that the economy grew modestly in September 1990. The recession we 'had to have' was nothing but a statistical fluke.[20]

But journalists don't just report on luck – they are themselves subject to it. Luck affects which stories get written, which ones make it into the news, and whether a story fizzles or fires up. Because the media plays such a vital role, discussing modern politics without mentioning the media would be like a conversation about kangaroo numbers that ignored the existence of guns. It is to the Fourth Estate that I now turn.

8

GAFFES, LEAKS AND SUPERFICIALITY – LUCK AND THE MEDIA

In the 1993 election, opposition leader John Hewson was interviewed by Channel Nine's Mike Willesee. Willesee asked a simple question about Hewson's plan to introduce a goods and services tax: will a birthday cake cost more or less? For the next minute, Hewson twisted and turned, explaining that it depended on the current sales tax arrangements, whether the cake was decorated and whether it had candles on it. Willesee ended with, 'If the answer to a birthday cake is so complex, you do have an overall problem with the GST, don't you?'[1]

Keen to make the most of the incident, Prime Minister Paul Keating decided to visit a bakery. He asked Peter Knott, Labor's candidate in the seat of Gilmore, to arrange a visit to one in Nowra. Unfortunately, Knott and the media team failed to check the background of the owner, who turned out to be a Liberal Party supporter. As the television cameras rolled, the bakery owner berated Keating over the issue of payroll tax, until the prime minister finally left the bakery.

Within twenty-four hours, a pair of media incidents had ensured that both candidates for prime minister had cake on their faces. In both cases, it is easy to see how fortune could have tipped things another way. Hewson had turned down many one-on-one interviews in the 1993 campaign, and could easily have rejected Willesee.[2] For his part, Keating simply experienced the bad luck of an advance team that failed to sniff out that they were about to walk into enemy territory. As Figure 5 shows, the 1993 election was so close that either of these media events could have been decisive.

Figure 5: How the 1993 election result was reported (Photo: Andrew Meares)

More than ever before, media gaffes can change the outcome of a political race. In the 2013 election, Jaymes Diaz was the Coalition candidate for Greenway, a seat held by Labor with a slim 0.9% margin. With the Liberal Party surging in public opinion, he agreed to an interview with Channel Ten's John Hill.[3]

'We have a six-point plan to make sure that we do stop the boats,' said Diaz.

'Six points, could you run through them for us?' the reporter replied.

'Well, I can run through all the details of the points, but look, the main thing is . . .,' responded Diaz.

A political reporter focused on the national story might have stopped there. After all, Diaz wasn't a party leader, he was a marginal seat candidate. Did anyone really care whether he knew the six-point plan?

But Hill wasn't a standard political reporter. He had reported on crime and New South Wales politics (which at times melded into the same story). As he later put it, 'I never ask candidates powder-puff questions and I decided beforehand to talk about policy, and play devil's advocate. Politics is a contact sport and if they want to play first grade, they ought to be prepared to take a hit.'[4]

When Hill didn't get an answer, he again pressed Diaz to name the six points. And again. And again. Diaz had the bad luck to be interviewed by a reporter who was willing to repeat the question eight times. The interview was such a train wreck that it made global news, including on the popular *Daily Show* in the US. Then, rather than explain himself, Diaz went to ground. He lost the election.

The Diaz interview was reminiscent of Jeremy Paxman's 1997 interview of UK politician Michael Howard, in which Paxman asked the same question twelve times in succession. Paxman later said that after asking the question half a dozen times: 'I was about to move on to something else when a voice came into my ear saying that the next piece of tape wasn't cut and that I'd better carry on with the interview.' As Paxman recalls it, he couldn't think of anything else to ask, so continued pressing the same question.[5] A chance event in the BBC editing process turned out to be bad luck for Michael Howard, who was made to appear as though he was concealing the truth (regarding an inquiry into prison escapes) from the viewers.

Other politicians can point to media moments that transformed their careers. In 2005, New South Wales opposition leader John Brogden was relishing his increased chances of winning the upcoming election, following the retirement of Premier Bob Carr. His wife was also expecting their second child. Then, at a late-night function, Brogden propositioned a woman at the bar. It was his bad luck that she turned out to be a *Sun-Herald* reporter, who wrote up the event.[6] Brogden resigned his position, and attempted suicide.

Major stories sometimes have chance beginnings. One of the Senate's fiercest inquisitors, Robert Ray, noticed that Mal Colston (a former Labor senator who had resigned to sit as an independent) had opened a conference on the Gold Coast, but claimed a travel allowance in Canberra for the same date. In a Senate inquiry, Ray asked a question about it. He recalls: 'The panic that then ensued was immense – three ministers lost their jobs, both the government and the opposition were massively embarrassed, a department was abolished, a deputy president was replaced.'[7] It was a major news story. As Ray concludes: 'One spear thrown on one day as an offhand comment led to that, so you need luck.'

Small errors can have unfortunate consequences. In 1991, Treasurer John Kerin resigned after a press conference in which he stumbled over the acronym 'GOS' (Gross Operating Surplus). In 2000, it was revealed that Howard government minister Peter Reith had passed the access code for his telephone calling card onto his son, who had given it to backpackers. Thousands of calls and a $50,000 bill later, tabloids were calling Reith 'Mr Ding A Ling'.[8] He retired at the next election. In 2006, opposition leader Kim Beazley confused television host Rove McManus with US presidential adviser Karl Rove. The mistake, which might once have been seen as a trivial error, precipitated a leadership challenge against Beazley by Kevin Rudd.

Sometimes, media attention changes the political debate when new information lands in the public domain. In 1987, a man with a radio scanner intercepted a car phone conversation between federal front-bencher Andrew Peacock and Victorian Liberal leader Jeff Kennett, in which Peacock described then federal opposition leader John Howard as a 'f--ing c--t'.[9] In 2005, Channel Nine reporter David Broadbent was leaked the Victorian budget. Reporting it, he joked that he was the real victim of the leak, since he'd been obliged 'to read it twice'. In every leak, there is some element of chance. As media commentator Rod Tiffen notes, leaking 'is surrounded by uncertainty and risk'.[10]

Recall from Chapter 6 that the expected tenure of a leader or opposition leader has fallen from six years in the 1960s to three years today. Former finance minister Lindsay Tanner argues that this has made the question of leadership a greater focus of the media – which in turn has helped to fuel more instability:

> The media are now unable to cope with reporting national politics outside an immediate election-campaign context without having an impending or actual leadership challenge to occupy them. Whichever party is struggling ... is ripe for a period of destabilisation that is actively encouraged by media outlets.

Prospective future challengers are carefully groomed and promoted. The Press Gallery can effectively anoint an individual as the Next Big Thing, and energetically promote that person as a future leader: inconsequential speeches become front-page news, and obscure preselection manoeuvres become signposts of future political ascendancy.[11]

The more unstable the leadership environment, the higher the odds that a chance media report will change history.

An important way in which luck affects reportage is by way of other events that happen during the day. As Annabel Crabb reflected to me, 'I will never forget a lady who said to me at a barbecue back when I'd just started as a journalist: "Isn't it amazing the way there's always just exactly enough news to fit in the paper?" It made me realise that people assume there is some sort of formula to news-gathering. And sometimes there is, but the capacity for random factors to affect what goes in the paper – and where it gets published – is almost infinite.'[12]

One economic study found that if a natural disaster hits a developing nation during a quiet news time, the country receives more foreign aid. Conversely, if a poor nation gets hit by a hurricane at a time when the rich world is engrossed in a celebrity court case, the victims will be doubly unlucky, since the story will likely be pushed down the news bulletins. One assessment finds that a disaster that occurs during the Olympics must have three times as many casualties as a disaster occurring on a regular news day to attract the same amount of foreign aid.[13]

Crabb noted another form of media timing: 'If you're a criminal or a dodgy politician or a disgraced sports star, you could possibly get off lightly if someone more famous than you is in trouble for similar reasons and has taken up the "crime spot" at the front of the paper. If someone very famous dies towards the end of the day, that'll work for you too.'[14] Conversely, blunders on quiet news days elicit maximum coverage. Prime Minister Tony Abbott's 2015 decision to knight Prince Philip would have been pilloried at any time of the year. But it attracted even more ridicule because the announcement was made on Australia Day, a time when little else was happening in the news.

There is also an element of luck in how persistently a journalist follows up a story. As noted, Jaymes Diaz had the misfortune to be interviewed by a reporter who kept pressing him when it became clear that he couldn't recall the Coalition's six-point plan. But the same factors affect whether a journalist decides to follow up a story after its first day. Annabel Crabb: 'Is the journalist concerned a dogged type, or a short-attention-span type? Is the journalist in good odour with the editor? Have they managed to get a photograph of you? If they have, I'm afraid you're in for a longer and more prominent ordeal. If they have photos of you smoking a ciggie and looking shifty, or trying to escape on a pushbike . . . you're toast.'[15]

Media slant can also be a matter of luck. Personal relationships between editors and politicians are subject to all the vagaries of any other sphere of life. For example, while media proprietors have typically leaned to the right, strong personal relationships have existed in the past between Labor treasurer Ted Theodore and Douglas Packer, between Tony Blair and Rupert Murdoch, and between Graham Richardson and Kerry Packer. The late Australian academic Jamie Mackie, who was one of Murdoch's classmates at Oxford, enjoyed reminiscing with friends about whether the course of history might have been different had Murdoch taken him up on his suggestion that they go to see Orson Welles' film *Citizen Kane*, the story of a megalomaniacal newspaper magnate who ends his life in bitter isolation.[16]

Murdoch's personal relationships have doubtless shaped his world view, but so too has chance played its part in his rise to power. When biographer Michael Wolff asked Rupert Murdoch why he had succeeded, Murdoch responded: 'Luck. There's just been a lot of luck.'[17]

◆

Earlier, I told the story of the Night of the Long Prawns, in which Senator Vince Gair was kept busy eating prawns and drinking alcohol, and failed to follow through with resigning from parliament so he could become an ambassador. The Gair affair has a media prelude.

Having secretly done the paperwork to appoint Gair as ambassador to Ireland, the Whitlam government intended the decision to remain secret until after he resigned from the Senate. Then, in March 1974, some days after the deal was done, federal cabinet met in Melbourne. Most of the parliamentary press gallery travelled there to cover the meeting. On a whim, thirty-year-old Laurie Oakes decided to stay in Canberra.

This meant that Oakes had to find something to write about. He began to make some phone calls – asking people about what was going on. Eventually, Oakes stumbled upon the fact that people were being coy about a particular diplomatic appointment. He thought about which non-government senator might be disgruntled enough to accept the job. Then, taking a guess, he made some more phone calls, asking his contacts, 'So, which job is Gair getting?' Their reactions confirmed the story, and Oakes broke the news.

The luck of Oakes having some extra time on his hands helped to shape one of the major events in the endgame of the Whitlam government. As veteran journalist Paul Kelly sums up his profession: 'Journalists live on luck and wits.'[18]

Until this point, I've discussed the role of luck in preselections and general elections, the careers of leaders, policy and the press. But what does all this mean for how we see the future? Should we – gasp – be a little more modest about what we think we spy in the political crystal ball?

9

PUNDITS, POLLSTERS AND PUNTERS – WHAT LUCK MEANS FOR FORECASTING

In June 2013, I was appearing live on ABC's *The Drum*, discussing political predictions. At the end of the segment, the host asked, 'Who will lead Labor into the 2013 election?' 'Julia Gillard,' I answered. Then she turned to the three people on her panel. One by one, Bruce Haigh, Fran Kelly and Peter Reith all predicted that Julia Gillard would remain prime minister.[1] Four predictions, all wrong. A fortnight later, Kevin Rudd replaced Julia Gillard as prime minister, and he led Labor to the 2013 election.

As pundits, we had egg on our faces. But the prediction error was the perfect illustration of the research that I was discussing. In a study titled 'The predictive power of political pundits: Prescient or pitiful?', Phillip Metaxas and I had assessed the performance of political insiders in predicting the future.[2] Analysing transcripts from two of Australia's most prominent Sunday talk shows – *Insiders* and *Meet the Press* – we searched for predictions that could turn out to be true or false.

We found twenty falsifiable predictions, of which thirteen turned out to be true – a hit rate of about two in three. Our study also uncovered a plethora of faux predictions, in which a commentator would say something definitive and then end with, 'Having said that, you can't rule out the possibility that something else might happen.'

Our conclusion was that forecasting should be done well, or not at all. If our commentators are going to talk about the future, then they should be held to account like weekend footy tipsters. This means asking questions with no wiggle room, such as 'Who will lead Labor into the 2013 election?' Then we can compare each expert's track record, and decide who to trust. Alternatively, if pundits are not willing to put their reputations on the line, then they should stick to discussing the past. Political experts are notoriously bad at forecasting. Six days before the 2004 federal election, one of the Sunday newspapers asked ten experts to forecast the result. Three thought Labor would win, while seven thought the Coalition would win, but with a reduced majority. None predicted the true result – a Coalition win with an *increased* majority.[3]

The largest ever study on political prediction was carried out by the University of Pennsylvania's Philip Tetlock, who asked 284 experts to make predictions about future events in the late 1980s and early 1990s.[4] By guaranteeing his participants anonymity, he was able to get them to make 27,450 separate predictions on questions such as whether the Soviet Union would collapse, whether Saddam Hussein would survive the first Gulf War, who would win the 1992 presidential election, and whether the NASDAQ share index would drop.

To test these predictions, Tetlock compared them to a naïve benchmark, which he called the 'chimp' approach. This allowed him to evaluate how well his expert commentators – many of

whom appeared regularly as television pundits – could forecast the future. It turned out that experts didn't beat the chimp:
political pundits were about as good at forecasting the future as
a team of dart-throwing monkeys.[5]

Other studies have reached similar conclusions. Analysing
nearly a thousand political predictions on the US television
show *The McLaughlin Group*, Nate Silver found that half of the
political predictions were correct and half incorrect. As he put
it, 'The panel may as well have been flipping coins.'[6]

The reason many pundit predictions do no better than this
is that politics is a chancy business. As renowned psychologist
Daniel Kahneman notes, 'The question is not whether these
experts are well trained. It is whether their world is predict-
able.'[7] And yet there do appear to be some systematic differences
among pundits in their style of thinking about the world.

Using the terminology of philosopher Isaiah Berlin, Philip
Tetlock drew a distinction between 'hedgehogs' and 'foxes'. As
he put it, 'intellectually aggressive hedgehogs knew one big
thing and sought, under the banner of parsimony, to expand
the explanatory power of that big thing to "cover" new cases;
the more eclectic foxes knew many little things and were con-
tent to improvise ad hoc solutions to keep pace with a rapidly
changing world.'[8] The foxes were more self-critical, less inclined
to become excessively enthusiastic about their own theories,
and more inclined to see how situations might tip in unexpected directions. Hedgehogs often said that something was a
certainty or an impossibility. Foxes tended to see the world in
shades of grey. In distinguishing between different groups of
experts, Tetlock's findings were clear: foxes consistently outper-
formed hedgehogs when it came to political judgement.

Unfortunately, people who know many little things can be less entertaining television talent than those who know one big thing. Nate Silver gives the example of Fox News commentator Dick Morris, a classic hedgehog pundit.[9] In 2005, Morris published a book titled *Condi vs Hillary: The next great presidential race*. Since then, he has variously predicted that George W. Bush's handling of Hurricane Katrina would boost his public standing, that Barack Obama would win Tennessee and Arkansas in 2008, and that Donald Trump had a 'damn good' chance of winning the Republican nomination in 2012. Each of these predictions turned out to be spectacularly wrong, but Morris remains entertaining, controversial and in high demand as a pundit.

Writer Dan Gardner argues that humans do not like the idea of events being random, and we want people who can peer into the future to tell us what will happen. As he puts it, 'confidence convinces'.[10] Our attraction to certainty in an uncertain world and our preference for confident experts exposes us to a paradox that both Tetlock and Gardner lament: the experts most likely to be sought after for predictions are those most likely to get it wrong.

Alongside this, many people are predisposed to rely on a single forecast. A simple rule of thumb is that if you have several estimates of something that is unknown or uncertain, then the average of those estimates is likely to be closer to the truth than any one estimate.[11] The average of economic forecasters outperforms a lone analyst. The average of sports pundits does better than a single expert. In a game of guessing the number of jellybeans in a jar, the average of all the guesses is closer to the truth than the vast majority of individual guesses. For example, one finance professor asked 102 students to guess the number of beans in a jar. The average of their estimates was closer to the true number than all but three of the individual guesses.[12]

This phenomenon – dubbed 'the wisdom of crowds' by writer James Surowiecki – isn't intuitive. In 1749, Leonhard Euler, one of the greatest mathematicians who ever lived, failed to solve a problem in astronomy because he refused to average the observations.[13] Euler thought the errors in each observation would multiply, not cancel each other out. And yet we have a plethora of evidence to show that more observations bring us closer to the truth. In the gameshow *Who Wants to be a Millionaire?*, audience members could either ask an expert or survey the audience members. The expert got the answer right 65% of the time – the audience majority got it right 91% of the time.[14]

The lesson from this research is that if you have to estimate the number of jellybeans in a jar, your best strategy is to look at the preceding guesses and write down the average. Likewise, rather than choosing among a dozen forecasters, you should take the average of their estimates. In both cases, the intuition is that each estimate contains some signal and some noise. By averaging, you cancel out some of the noise. So an average should have a little less luck and a little more wisdom than any individual estimate.

Unfortunately, one of the key metrics in politics – opinion-poll reporting – breaks this rule. By definition, each poll contains new information, and it is information that the media outlet has had to pay good money to obtain. So most opinion polls are reported on the front page of a newspaper as an event in themselves.

Alas, any one opinion poll is subject to sampling error. Suppose opinion pollsters knew everyone's phone number and we all agreed to answer their surveys. Even then, there would be a chance that their sample overrepresented Labor voters or overrepresented Coalition voters. In such an ideal poll, standard statistics tells us that one in every ten of their polls would miss the true result by more than 2 percentage points, and one in forty would be wrong by more than 3 percentage points.

So even a poll with a flawless sampling technique will sometimes be wide of the mark. But the problem is even worse in the real world. That's because survey companies don't know everyone's phone number, because some people aren't home when the pollster calls, and because many people hang up on pollsters. This means that even when there isn't much happening in politics, polls can jump around like a seismometer in an earthquake.

In 2006, polling company AC Nielsen conducted a monthly opinion poll for Fairfax newspapers, including the *Sydney Morning Herald*.[15] In April, it estimated Labor's two-party vote at 51%. In May, its estimate was 54%. And in June, its estimate was again 51%. It's worth pointing out that 54% is a huge share of the vote: not since 1977 has a government won such a large majority. So a poll that suggests someone is going to get 54% of the vote should be read with at least one raised eyebrow.

Unfortunately, that's not how the *Sydney Morning Herald* saw it. In May, it reported the rise from 51% to 54% with a front-page headline 'Voters spurn tax cuts and swing to ALP'. A month later, the June poll drop from 54% to 51% was reported on page one with a similarly breathless 'ALP vote falls after Beazley vow to workers'. Sadly, a more accurate story would have appeared deep inside the paper, perhaps with the caption 'Polls have errors, statisticians show'.

As call-centre costs continue to fall, polls are appearing with ever-greater frequency. Once an intermittent phenomenon, some Australian polls now appear fortnightly, and weekly during campaigns. In the US, Gallup conducts a daily political poll – boldly spruiking its results as 'The will of the people – every day'. As a politician, I've lost count of the number of times I've heard the question 'How do you feel about the latest poll results?' Whether it's up, down or sideways, my answer is always the same: 'Let's focus on the issues, not the polls.'

Yet just as luck plays a significant role in politics, it affects opinion polls. On election eve, Newspoll forecast the wrong party to win the 1998 election, while Morgan forecast the wrong winner in 2001. In a survey of the accuracy of opinion pollsters on election eve, political scientist Murray Goot concluded, 'Since 1993, when the pollsters began to report a two-party-preferred count, the average two-party-preferred error for the phone polls conducted by Newspoll has been 1.4, for Morgan 1.8 and for Nielsen 2 percentage points'.[16] So the average error for the median pollster is 1.8 percentage points.

As Goot points out, this might sound good until you realise that if you had set up a bogus polling firm, which did no surveys but simply predicted that the result in every election would be a dead heat, then that polling firm would have a two-party error of 1.8 percentage points. In other words, a dart-throwing monkey could produce as good a track record as the typical pollster on election eve. And polls conducted earlier than this have even larger errors. For example, those conducted a year before the election have average errors of around 4 percentage points.[17]

None of this is surprising. One problem for pollsters is that voting patterns are never stable: my research shows that about 10% of us change our vote from one election to the next.[18] The other problem is that reporters rarely acknowledge how error-prone their polls are. Although the sampling error is sometimes noted in small print at the foot of an article in Australia, it rarely makes its way into the text.

By contrast, the best US papers take a much more careful approach, explicitly noting the statistical margin of error when discussing the results. This can be done without needless jargon. For example, a sentence in the *New York Times* might read: 'The Times poll showed the race to be deadlocked, with neither candidate holding a lead beyond the margin of sampling error.'

This is particularly important when we're dealing with polls whose sampling technique isn't flawless. Analysing polls in the 2004 election, Justin Wolfers and I estimated that the true margin of error for Australian opinion polls might be three or four times as large as the pollsters assume.[19] That suggests that there's a lot of luck – or statistical noise – in poll results.

Another factor to remember is that the sampling error when comparing two polls is larger still, since both polls have their own margins of error. When we compare a single poll with the actual result, it's like a drunkard grabbing onto a lamppost: sometimes he gets it, sometimes he misses. But when we compare two polls, it's like a pair of drunks trying to shake hands: the odds that they'll line up exactly with reality are slim indeed.

The bottom line is that changes in polls from one week to another are even more error-prone than the polls themselves. So statements like 'since the last poll, the Coalition's vote share is up 2%' should be taken with a handful of salt.

The question of who is going to win the next election is not the most interesting one in politics. But if you want to know the answer, there are several approaches that are superior to using a single poll.

One way is to average across several polls. Just as looking for small differences can be a problem, averaging across many polls is a partial solution.[20] It happens too infrequently because it requires a measure of modesty that we rarely see in media proprietors – a recognition that their competitors might have insights that they lack, and that their 'scoop' might not be error-free. Thankfully, those with an interest in pooled polls can find United States figures at Nate Silver's FiveThirtyEight website, and Australian estimates at William Bowe's Poll Bludger website.

If you're a poll addict who's willing to switch drugs, you might consider switching from polls that ask 'Who would you vote for?' to polls that ask 'Who do you think will win?' In a recent analysis, economists Justin Wolfers and David Rothschild demonstrate that asking about expectations rather than intentions produces estimates that are considerably closer to the actual result.[21] They give the example of the 2008 presidential election, where Barack Obama led John McCain in all expectations polls, but not in voting intentions polls. Similarly, in the 2012 Republican presidential primary race, standard voting intentions polls were variously led by Donald Trump, Rick Perry, Herman Cain, Newt Gingrich and Rick Santorum. By contrast, polls that asked 'Who do you think will win the nomination?' constantly predicted Mitt Romney.

When Wolfers and Rothschild look at a handful of Australian election polls, they find that expectations polls pick the correct winner nine times out of ten, while intentions polls pick the winner correctly only four times out of ten.[22] This suggests that people who based their election forecasts on standard opinion polls would be wrong most of the time, while those who based their forecasts on expectations polls would have been right almost all of the time.

Why do expectations polls produce a more accurate forecast? The researchers argue that asking people who is likely to win is akin to expanding the sample size by a factor of twenty. Each person in an expectations poll is effectively telling the researchers how twenty of their friends and family would vote. Expectations polls act as a force multiplier – effectively allowing a sample of 1000 people to tap into the views of 20,000 people.

So, if you're addicted to polls, you should pool them. If you're willing to try a new drug, you should use expectations polls. But what about if you were willing to kick the habit: to go poll turkey? If only there was a better alternative . . .

A week before the 1983 election, Malcolm Fraser was being interviewed on the ABC's *Four Corners* program by a panel of journalists. Despite struggling in the campaign, Fraser kept up a brave face. The exchange went as follows.[23]

PETER BOWERS: How do you rate your chances of still being prime minister after next Saturday?

MALCOLM FRASER: It will be to the judgment of the Australian people. But many Australians are gamblers on the racecourse, and I suppose with the poker machines. The Labor Party would be the biggest gamble in history – with their children, their families. I don't think Australians are going to take that gamble.

PETER BOWERS: You wouldn't like a little bet on it, would you?

Even Fraser couldn't suppress a chuckle.

Election betting markets (also known as 'prediction markets') can be traced back to at least the nineteenth century. Street-corner bookmakers – some of them literally sitting on the curb of Wall Street – offered odds on US presidential races. These odds were frequently reported in our newspapers, which also detailed election odds for British and Australian elections.[24] To peruse papers of the era is to come across headings such as this one in the *Age* of 1924: 'Election eve: The betting market'. After World War II, opinion polls became ubiquitous, and betting markets faded away. But in recent years, election betting markets have returned to many countries.

Using data from these markets, researchers in Australia, Germany, Sweden and the United States have compared the predictive power of voting intention polls and betting markets.[25] Every time, betting markets have been found to perform at least as well as, and usually better than, the polls. This even holds true for the historical election betting markets, with the odds from those markets having been shown to be an accurate predictor of the results in the 1884 to 1928 US presidential elections.[26]

Another advantage of betting markets is that they cover a wide range of outcomes and are updated immediately. Recent Australian elections have seen election betting markets on the headline result, individual electorate results, the election date and leadership contenders. Like share prices, betting odds are in real time, so if a sudden event takes place, the response is immediate.

If you believe that there's a lot of luck in politics, then you should be naturally sceptical of people who tell you that they can forecast the result. As I noted at the outset, politics is more like poker than chess, and few people believe they can confidently predict this year's winner of the World Series of Poker.

For those who must play the forecasting game, poll pooling, expectations polls and betting markets offer a more reliable gauge of the future than the standard approach of looking at one-off opinion polls. The advantage of each of these approaches is that they are less volatile than a standard front-page poll. If the typical opinion poll were a television character, it would be Kramer from *Seinfeld*.

Taking out the random variation makes the horse race of politics less interesting. This is no bad thing, since it creates more space to discuss ideas about the future. Elections are not just about choosing a party to lead the country. They also provide a chance to talk about the great nation-building project; what makes us proud and what needs changing. Less reporting of error-prone opinion polls might create space for a deeper national conversation about the kind of country we aspire to be in the future.

Putting luck in the picture should make us look differently at forecasting. But that's just the beginning. Let's now turn to some of the other ways thinking about luck shapes how economists, political scientists and policymakers see the nature of politics.

10

GENEROSITY, FAILING FAST AND HYPERPARTISANSHIP – WHAT ARE THE LESSONS FROM LUCK?

In 1964, Lyndon Johnson signed the US Civil Rights Act, fully conscious of its electoral consequences for the Democratic Party, but knowing it would make life better for millions of black Americans. In 1978, Deng Xiaoping allowed private farming experiments in Anhui province that would eventually bring hundreds of millions of Chinese out of poverty. With his 1992 Redfern Park Speech to a predominantly Indigenous audience, Paul Keating became the first Australian leader to acknowledge that, 'We committed the murders. We took the children from their mothers. We practiced discrimination and exclusion.'

The point of this book is not to persuade you that politics is all luck. Some of the turning points in world history have come about through the tenacity and ingenuity of great politicians. Legislation can save lives. Speeches can change minds. While most politicians in the world are decent and hard-working, some are corrupt and lazy. If I believed that every political event was the result of a dice roll, I wouldn't be in politics.

And yet luck matters. In this book, I've presented evidence

that luck affects parties, candidates and leaders. Whether it's a rainy polling day or a global slump, a bad ballot draw or beautiful genes, luck shapes the outcomes of politics. In each case, chance is indifferent to whether the victim or beneficiary is from the left, right or centre.

But when it comes to crediting the role of luck, a strong pattern emerges. One of the curious facts about luck is that those who believe in it are more likely to be from the left than the right. With some exceptions, progressive politicians are more likely to think that luck matters. Conservative politicians are more likely to reject the role of luck. US economist Robert Frank goes so far as to suggest that luck makes a useful litmus test for political ideology: 'If you don't know where a new acquaintance stands politically, just ask him about this. If he insists luck doesn't matter, he's almost surely a staunch conservative.'[1]

The tendency of those on the right to reject luck can be seen in the self-help and get-rich-quick literature. In his 1937 book *Think and Grow Rich*, Napoleon Hill argues that those who suffer poverty 'are the creators of their own misfortunes'. A belief in bad luck, he says, gets picked up by your subconscious mind, and then causes you to fail. And just as Hill thinks the poor are to blame for their poverty, he argues that 'Riches come ... in response to definite demands, based upon the application of definite principles, and not by chance or luck'.[2]

Similarly, as Wayne Dwyer puts it in *Staying on the Path*, 'Everything that is happening is supposed to be happening'.[3] Or in the words of Mihaly Csikszentmihalyi, 'The more psychic energy we invest in the future of life, the more we become a part of it.'[4]

Doubtless it's easier to believe in destiny when you occupy the corner office than when you're squatting under a bridge.

But you don't have to be poor to recognise that luck matters. Underpinning the old-fashioned notion of *noblesse oblige* was a sense that if you're one of those to whom much has been given, then you have a correspondingly larger obligation to society. As the sixteenth-century religious reformer John Bradford put it, 'there, but for the grace of God, go I'.

In her book on luck, Esther Eidinow contrasts the inaugural addresses of George W. Bush and Barack Obama.[5] Bush sees the future in certain terms, both for the nation ('We go forward with complete confidence in the eventual triumph of freedom') and for individuals (each citizen is to be given 'his or her own destiny'). By contrast, Obama leaves more to chance, painting a picture of an uncertain future, shaped by 'risk-takers' with a responsibility to the legacy left by previous generations.

A similar pattern emerges across countries. Continental Europeans are typically regarded as more left-wing than the citizens of English-speaking countries. A majority of Germans, Italians and Greeks believe that success depends on forces outside our control, while a majority of British and American respondents disagree.[6] Compared with those in the United States and Britain, people in continental Europe are twice as likely to say that luck matters for getting ahead. A greater belief in luck is one reason why the social safety net in continental Europe is more generous than it is in Anglo nations.

Within Australia, a survey asked people whether success in life was determined more by 'hard work', or by 'luck and connections'. While 19% of Coalition voters believed that luck mattered more than hard work, the figure was 31% for Labor voters.[7]

When the new federal members of parliament delivered their first speeches in 2013, it was Liberal parliamentarian

Christian Porter who opined that 'with effort almost anything is possible'. On the other side of the House, Labor member Tim Watts noted the obligation to help 'good people with the bad luck' to live under oppressive regimes.

There's wisdom in both of these perspectives. Effort really does matter. At the centre of capitalism is the idea that if you work harder, you will be rewarded. In modern-day Australia, it's obvious that some people put in more effort than others. As a parent, I'm fascinated by the work on 'grit' by psychologist Angela Duckworth and her co-authors. This research shows that an inner drive to persevere is one of the most powerful predictors of success in life.[8] Most of the deeply satisfying things in life aren't enjoyable the first time (chocolate, sex and television being the most obvious exceptions). To become highly proficient at a job, sport or hobby requires gritty practice – a willingness to persevere through the initial setbacks.

As aphorist Coleman Cox said in 1922, 'I am a great believer in luck. The harder I work, the more of it I seem to have.'[9] Yet the 'pull yourself up by your bootstraps' perspective risks ignoring the many ways that chance shapes people's lives. Analysing income differences across the globe, the economist Branko Milanović estimates that three-fifths of the variation is due to country of birth, and another one-fifth is due to parents' social status.[10] In other words, at least four-fifths of the variation in earnings across the world is due to the accident of birth. A hard-working person born in Nepal is likely to earn a lower income than a lazy person born in Norway.

As a young child, I attended school in Banda Aceh, at the northern tip of the Indonesian island of Sumatra. It was an extraordinary experience for a kindergartener, and one that reminded me of how lucky I was in comparison with my class-mates, many of whom lived in homes without running water and went to bed hungry, with no protection from malarial mosquitoes. It was easy to see how nineteenth-century min-ing magnate Cecil Rhodes had said, while living in Africa, 'Remember that you are an Englishman, and have conse-quently won first prize in the lottery of life.'

Harvard philosopher John Rawls proposed a thought exper-iment of a 'veil of ignorance', which asks you to imagine yourself as an unborn child. What kind of society would you want if you didn't know whether you would be born male or female, rich or poor, plain or handsome, with a disability or without? From behind the veil of ignorance, most people tend to prefer a social safety net that is more generous to the vulnerable, and often opt for more egalitarianism than we see in today's society.

We can take a similar approach to thinking about unforeseen events. If you believe cruel 'shafts of fate' can strike anyone – that a debilitating accident or a company going insolvent can change lives – then you are probably likely to support a more compas-sionate approach to those who are the victims of bad luck.

If I've persuaded you that luck matters in politics, then I hope I've also convinced you that the way we view politicians today gives too much credit to the victors and too little to the losers. If we accept that we live in a chance-filled world, we might instead be more sceptical of claims to sole ownership of success and more sympathetic to those who've flopped.

It isn't just about cruelty towards those who are merely unlucky. There's also a risk that if we denigrate the unsuccess-ful, we miss out on the insights that come from slipping on life's banana peels. One illustration of this comes from an experiment designed to simulate the share market. Students were brought into a computer lab and asked to trade with one another on an artificial market. The shares were designed to perform as they do in real life, and students were told that if they did well on the game, they would get real money.

As economist Megan McArdle describes it, the result was a bubble.[11] Students paid too much for assets, they rose in value, and then their price crashed. Only after three rounds of playing the game did students learn to avoid bubbles. But this only works if the same people are kept in the game. If students are taken out between rounds and replaced with new participants, the bubble markets keep recurring. Firing people after a bad series of trades ends up creating an unstable share market.

The benefits of failure are recognised in innovative industry clusters such as in Silicon Valley. As technology entrepreneur Erica Zidel notes, 'In the start-up world, failure is almost synonymous with learning experience . . . Being a founder who has failed before signals to the community that, one, you've done this before, and, two, you've gathered information on what doesn't work and are better armed to create something that does.'[12] Another technology entrepreneur, Kamran Elahian, famously drove a car whose numberplate bore the name of his first failed company, Momenta.[13]

F. Scott Fitzgerald may have said there are no second acts in American lives, but in Silicon Valley success often happens only in act two. Mottos such as 'fail fast' and 'fail smart' reflect the philosophy that even geniuses will sometimes bomb out. The key is to minimise the losses and try to learn from failure.

A similar philosophy underpins new thinking in sports coaching. In an attempt to minimise the high dropout rate from youth sports, a philosophy known as 'positive coaching' has emerged. At its core is the idea that athletes control just three things: their level of effort, whether they learn from experiences, and how they respond to mistakes.[14] Positive coaching is about providing better feedback to athletes, so that they can hone their technique. It focuses on using moments of disappointment – a missed shot on goal, a bungled pass, even a bad official's call – as 'teachable moments'. Where old-style coaching worries about winning today's game at all costs, positive coaching thinks about using today's mistakes to do better tomorrow.

Not only entrepreneurs and sports coaches can learn from failure. United States president Franklin Delano Roosevelt suffered painfully in his personal life, losing the use of both his legs through polio. As president in the Great Depression, Roosevelt saw government as being about learning from mistakes. His approach to governing, Roosevelt famously said, would be one of 'bold, persistent experimentation'. In one of his 1933 fireside chats, he candidly outlined what this would mean:

> I do not deny that we may make mistakes of procedure as we carry out the policy. I have no expectation of making a hit every time I come to bat. What I seek is the highest possible batting average, not only for myself but for the team. Theodore Roosevelt once said to me: 'If I can be right 75% of the time, I shall come up to the fullest measure of my hopes.'[15]

Franklin Roosevelt is generally regarded as the best United States president of the twentieth century.[16]

One of the reasons Abraham Lincoln and Winston Churchill were both such successful leaders for their nations in times of adversity was that they had suffered failure earlier in their careers. In Australia, our two longest-serving prime ministers – Robert Menzies and John Howard – were ignominiously dumped by their colleagues as party leaders. Both returned as better leaders.

Menzies subsequently reflected on his first period as leader: 'I do not doubt that my knowledge of people, and how to get along with them and persuade them, lagged behind ... I had yet to acquire the common touch, to learn that human beings are delightfully illogical but mostly honest, and to realise that all-black and all-white are not the only hues in the spectrum.'[17] Similarly, Howard says of his early misfortune, 'You become a better listener, a better consultant, a better advocate ... you can smell problems coming better. And finally being successful and entrenched, you realise that some of the things you became nervous about in the past were not really big issues at all.'[18]

As we have seen, bad luck – in the form of the Canberra air disaster – was part of the reason Menzies lost his party's leadership in 1941. But this setback ultimately made him a better prime minister. As a community, we need to do a better job of recognising the role of failure in success. If we raise the price of failure too high, we may sacrifice the 'teachable moments' that follow a bout of bad judgement – and bad luck. As innovator Steve Jobs once reflected, 'Near-death experiences can help one see more clearly sometimes.'[19]

Recognising the role of luck in politics is also important for understanding what works on the hustings. A campaigner who thinks that politics is a game of chess rather than poker may erroneously believe that they can control the world around them. This can lead to serious mistakes, as well as some seriously odd results.

Here's an analogy. In a famous experiment conducted by B.F. Skinner, a hungry pigeon in a cage was presented with food at random intervals.[20] It quickly learned to associate the arrival of the food with whatever it was doing when the food arrived. Not realising that the timing of the food was a matter of pure chance, the bird acted as though there was a causal relationship between its behaviour and the arrival of the food. One pigeon repeatedly turned anti-clockwise. Another thrust its head into the top of the cage. One bird made incomplete pecking movements towards the floor. Another developed a pendulum motion. Each bird appeared to be convinced that it was doing the thing that would make the food appear.

It may sound ridiculous to suggest that campaign hands make the same errors as Skinner's pigeons. And yet the old style of campaigning suffered from precisely this problem. Strategists variously advocate that you should always attack your opponent, always ignore your opponent, look stern, look cheery, stand on street corners waving a sign, or even drive around in a car with a roof-mounted megaphone. Because campaigners get limited feedback, they often persist with the equivalent of anti-clockwise turns and pecking movements. Or, like the Monopoly players in Chapter 1 who were randomly assigned to be lucky or unlucky, they become arrogant when fortune goes their way.

One piece of folk wisdom is that Australian governments always win their second election. While it is true that no one-term federal government has been ousted since 1932, a closer look at the data reveals several first-time governments which suffered near-death experiences. In the last four 'honeymoon' elections – 1974, 1984, 1998 and 2010 – the average swing against the government was 2.4%. In one of those elections (1998), the government won a minority of the vote. In another (2010), the government won a minority of the seats. A careful analysis of the data suggests that the so-called honeymoon effect has more to do with luck than skill.

With the advent of data-driven campaigning – popularised in books such as *Get Out the Vote* and *The Victory Lab* – gut feeling is finally being replaced by careful statistics. Such methods help solve the problem because they start from the presumption that a given campaign technique doesn't work. The philosophy of 'prove it' lays down a challenge to campaigners: sift out the luck and demonstrate that your strategy can make a difference to the election outcome. Consequently, campaigners who understand the role of luck tend to be more modest and more effective than those who do not.

Another implication of luck is that it should make us look more sceptically at excessive partisanship. To extremists – people my colleague Jim Chalmers calls 'hyperpartisans' – those on the opposite side of a debate are not simply wrong, they are amoral, venal and dishonest.[21] As Chalmers puts it, hyperpartisanship elevates 'combat over problem-solving', and feeds on 'polls, slogans, trivia, extremism'. Hyperpartisans don't just disagree with their political opponents – they hate them.

Luck should make us even more concerned about extreme partisanship, since the political environment can act to magnify small gaps into large differences. Recall the Stanford Prison experiment, where the toss of a coin decided whether a participant would play a student or a guard. Yet within days, those randomly appointed guards were abusing and 'sadistically tormenting' those who had been randomly designated prisoners.

Similarly, the erosion of a political middle ground can mean that small chance events end up having large consequences. Imagine a landscape covered with balls, each of which represents a person's ideology. If the ground is flat, then it doesn't matter much if a ball is placed a little to the left or right. But if the ground is hilly, then small perturbations end up making a big difference. If a ball starts on the top of a steep hill, a small change in its placement will greatly affect where it ends up.

Moving from moderation to hyperpartisanship is like going from a flat political landscape to a hilly one. Not only is it harder to see eye to eye, but the luck of a person's starting point exacerbates trivial differences into mammoth gaps. A recent analysis of media releases put out by members of the US Congress found that one-quarter used exaggerated language to deride the opposition or their ideas.[22] Attempts to undermine the legitimacy of individuals has manifested in the claim by 'birthers' on the extreme right that President Barack Obama was not born in the United States, and by birthers on the extreme left that Prime Minister Tony Abbott did not properly renounce his claim to British citizenship.

The partisan gap in the United States has been systematically measured by political scientists Keith Poole and Howard Rosenthal, who use congressional votes to place each legislator on the political spectrum.[23] They show that during the interwar period, the gap between the average Democrat and the average Republican narrowed considerably. In the 1940s, half of all legislators were what they classify as 'moderates'.

As Figure 6 shows, the gap between the major political parties then began to grow. Today, partisanship in the US House of

Representatives is higher than at any time since the late 1800s. At the same time as the gap has grown, the share of moderates has fallen – from above half to just one in ten. Across US counties, the same pattern can be seen. From 1976 to 2008, the share of Americans living in a 'landslide county' – where the incumbent had more than a 20% margin – rose from 27% to 48%.[24]

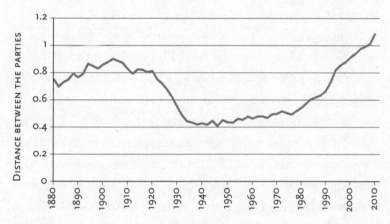

Figure 6: Partisan gap in the US House of Representatives
Source: voteview.com

In Australia, strict party discipline prevents a similar analysis of our partisan gap. However, it is possible to look at the gap in another way. Since 1996, researchers at the Australian National University have surveyed voters and candidates, asking them to place themselves on a left–right scale running from 0 to 10.[25]

Figure 7 shows that the ideological gap between Labor and Coalition voters has grown over the past two decades. For voters, the partisan gap has increased from 1.5 to 2.1. For candidates, the partisan gap has increased from 2.4 to 3.3.

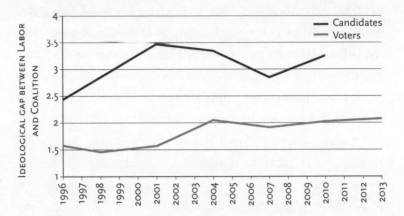

Figure 7: Partisan gap among Australian voters and candidates

Another measure of partisanship is the share of 'crossover' candidates – either Labor candidates who are to the right of the average Coalition candidate, or Coalition candidates who are to the left of the average Labor candidate. In 1996, one in ten candidates fitted this description. By 2010, it was down to almost one in twenty.

From the late 1960s to the mid-1980s, Liberal MP Bert Kelly wrote a 'Modest Member' column for the *Australian Financial Review*. In 2012, the newspaper revived the 'Modest Member' column, this time written in turn by a group of Liberal Party parliamentarians.[26] Analysing the columns from both eras, I estimate that 36% of the original 'Modest Member' columns criticised the Labor Party, while 29% criticised the Coalition. By contrast, the new 'Modest Member' columns criticise the Labor Party 70% of the time, but criticise the Coalition less than 2% of the time. Today's 'Modest Members' are twice as likely to censure their political opponents, but fourteen times less likely to find fault with those on their own side.

The same pattern can be seen in an increasingly polarised media. From 1985 to 2013, the share of Americans who say that the press tends to favour one side rose from 53% to 76%.[27] The rise of Fox News on the right and MSNBC on the left reflects a pattern in which media outlets are more likely to be critics or cheerleaders than straight reporters.[28]

A number of careful research papers have shown that slanted media reporting has the power to shape political views. In one study, researchers used the fact that the cable television rollout of Fox News in the US in the late 1990s was a staggered one. Comparing towns with and without Fox News, they observed that Fox boosted the Republican vote by 0.4 to 0.7 percentage points, suggesting that up to one-quarter of Fox viewers switched their vote as a consequence of watching the channel.[29]

The rising partisan gap matters because of the power of party loyalty. One experiment recruited Republican and Democratic partisans.[30] They were read statements in which both the 2004 presidential candidates reversed their position. In George Bush's case, the reversal related to his support for Enron chief Ken Lay, while in John Kerry's case, the backflip related to the sustainability of social security.

The partisans, it turned out, had little difficulty in letting their own candidate off the hook. Perhaps the Republicans thought that Bush could never have known about Lay's culpability, while Democrats thought that the facts on social security had changed.

This experiment also had a twist. Participants were asked to engage in their political task while lying in an fMRI scanner, while the researchers looked at their brain activity. As a partisan processed a backflip by their candidate, the experimenters found

that the most active regions of the brain were those typically associated with emotional activity, particularly a region called the
cingulate, which activates when we forgive someone. Meanwhile,
the parts of the brain involved in what neuroscientists call 'cold
reasoning' were fairly quiet. Partisanship, it turns out, is predominantly an emotional activity, not an intellectual one.

Another experiment asked students to rate a hypothetical
social welfare program. The article described the program, and
said whether Republican or Democratic leaders supported it.
The researcher found that what mattered was party leaders'
views, not the policy itself.[31] So long as the Democratic leadership supported it, Democratic voters would back a harsh
welfare program. So long as the Republican leadership liked it,
Republican voters would support a lavish welfare program.

Asked why they formed their views, participants denied
that they had been influenced by the views of party leaders. Of
course they weren't swayed by the partisan tag, they assured the
researchers. Each individual was convinced they had formed a
view after carefully analysing the merits of the policy.

Perhaps it isn't surprising that we want to accept the views of
people we like. In a famous experiment in the 1950s, psychologist Solomon Asch asked eight people in a room to estimate the
length of a line on a piece of paper.[32] After thinking about the
question, each person took it in turns to say their answer aloud.

The question itself was easy. When a control group was
asked to answer it in a room on their own, 99% of respondents
got it right. But the Asch experiment had a twist. The first
seven participants were actors, who deliberately gave the wrong
answer. The only answer the experimenter cared about was the
person on the end: would they conform or get it right? It turned

out that in one-third of cases, the participant on the end chose conformity and gave an incorrect answer.

The evidence on groupthink poses a challenge to the way we often think about politics. The standard Enlightenment view is that reason will ultimately prevail and that providing more information will moderate the views of extremists. And yet there is some evidence that the opposite might be true. In one laboratory study, participants were asked their views on two controversial topics: affirmative action and gun control.[33] They were then provided with perspectives on both topics. Rather than becoming more centrist, the researchers found that participants disputed contrary ideas, and uncritically accepted supporting ideas. Given a chance to search for more information, participants sought out three times as many arguments from supporting sources as from sources that contradicted their beliefs. By the end of the exercise, participants' views were more extreme than when they began.

Strikingly, the more politically knowledgeable a person is to begin with, the better they were able to refute contrary ideas and use supporting facts to bolster their view. This accords with another study that asked people to write down their view on a social problem, and then to list arguments for or against that view.[34] Not surprisingly, the more educated were the participants, the more arguments they listed. But this only held true for favourable arguments. More education had no effect on the number of contrary arguments that people came up with. As psychologist Jonathan Haidt explains it, 'people invest their IQ in buttressing their own case rather than in exploring the entire issue more fully and evenhandedly'.[35] Once group loyalties are engaged, he argues, 'you can't change people's minds by utterly refuting their arguments'.[36]

Hyperpartisanship can be destructive. In Figure 8, I show the share of Labor and Coalition voters who say that they 'strongly dislike' the opposing party (meaning that on a 0 to 10 scale, they rate that party a 0).[37] Since the late 1990s, the share of people who hate their opponents has risen from under one in six voters to over one in four voters.

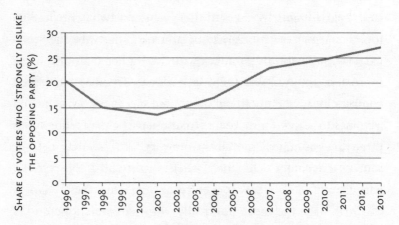

Figure 8: Share of voters who strongly dislike the opposing party

A similar pattern can be seen in the United States. Since the 1970s, surveys have asked people to assign a rating to the major parties. Over that time, people's average rating of their own party has stayed constant, but their rating of the opposite party has halved.[38] To give some sense of the distaste with which people view those on the other side, Republicans and Democrats are more hostile to one another than Catholics are towards Protestants, Democrats are towards big business, and Republicans are towards gay men and lesbians. Partisans regard those in the other party as less intelligent, more selfish and more closed-minded.

Surveys have also explored people's attitudes to cross-party marriages. In 1960, just 5% of Americans said they would be displeased if their son or daughter married outside their political party. By 2010, 41% said they would be unhappy at such a prospect.[39] Americans are more disturbed by cross-party marriages than by interracial marriages.[40] The typical American parent is more troubled by a cross-party marriage than learning that their child is gay.[41] So large is the partisan gap in the United States that marriage across party lines is now a greater taboo than miscegenation or homosexuality.

An intriguing experiment set out to test the implications of partisan attitudes by asking participants to assign a university scholarship to two hypothetical candidates, each with a background in a political party's youth wing.[42] When given a partisan cue, participants tended to give the scholarship to someone with their own political leanings – even if the other candidate was better qualified. The researchers also found that discrimination based on partisanship was stronger than discrimination based on race.

Partisanship shows up in unexpected places. Under the prime ministerships of Margaret Thatcher and Tony Blair, the same cat – Humphrey – lived in 10 Downing Street. Yet when shown a picture and asked to give Humphrey an 'approval rating', Labour partisans were nearly twice as likely to approve of the moggie if he was described as 'Tony Blair's cat' than if he was described as 'Margaret Thatcher's cat'.[43] Another study found that Barack Obama's dog, Bo, received a lower rating from people who disliked President Obama.

Psychology teaches us that partisanship is not merely a rational process – it's also an emotional one. The group loyalties that bind together political supporters can build a sense of *esprit de corps*, but they can also make hyperpartisans deaf to the wisdom of their opponents. Troublingly, more education and more time to research the topic seem to cause partisans to further entrench their positions, rather than moderate their ideas.

I've been a member of the Labor Party all my adult life, but that doesn't mean I regard people in other political parties as corrupt, unscrupulous or stupid. It worries me when I see the Australian partisan gap widening, the dislike of opposing parties rising, and more energy being devoted to hating than creating. When four-tenths of Americans would shun a son-in-law or daughter-in-law because they support a different party, we know partisanship is out of control.

The bigger partisan differences become, the more luck matters. In a political system with mutual respect and plenty of centrist candidates, the consequences of a lucky victory are slight. But when parties are polarised, and partisan dislike is high, luck converts tiny initial variations into divergent outcomes. As in the analogy of balls scattered across a surface, the degree to which the luck of a starting point matters depends on how uneven the surface is. Australia's electoral topography is hilly, and getting hillier. The further apart our parties become, the more that the luck of politics sees small differences magnified into wildly distinct endpoints.

Understanding the role of luck in politics isn't just a question that should interest political scientists. Recognising the importance of luck can profoundly alter the way in which all of us think about politics. Putting luck back at the centre of politics should help us build a system that makes it possible to learn from failure. We do this in other spheres of life. At its best, our health system guards against the bad luck of sickness, our unemployment system protects against the bad luck of job loss, and farm assistance absorbs some of the bad luck of drought. We have policies like these not merely because we don't want people to suffer, but also because our society recognises the waste inherent in losing the skills of the unlucky. For the same reason, we need a politics that does not throw the unlucky onto the scrap heap. Some of history's greatest leaders suffered unfortunate setbacks in their early careers. But the bad luck that befell them ultimately served to make them more effective politicians.

Understanding how luck affects politics ought to make us particularly concerned about the rise in partisanship. If parties a generation ago were akin to groups chatting in the centre of the town square, today they are more like teams shouting from the edges of the square. Extreme partisanship threatens the notion of politics as a communal conversation, and raises the risk of people being confined to increasingly extreme echo chambers.

Intolerance of failure and the rise of partisanship are trends that favour populists over long-game reformers. Consequently, those who believe that we should learn from mistakes have a tougher time of it than in the past. The principle that we should disagree without being disagreeable is under threat.

11

WHAT IF?

The novel *Idlewild* tells the story of an America that has been tweaked in two small ways.[1] In 1962, Marilyn Monroe's housekeeper, Eunice Murray, is persuaded to check on her in the evening. Discovering the star comatose, she calls an ambulance, and Monroe makes a full recovery. Then, in 1963, Lee Harvey Oswald's second bullet hits John F. Kennedy's skull one inch further to the side. Dallas doctors are able to save his life.

The most intriguing part of *Idlewild* is its discussion of the subsequent legacies of Monroe and Kennedy. Monroe spends the 1960s and 1970s embroiled in litigation and struggling to get over her drug addiction. In 1982, she stars in a dramatisation of the Dostoevsky novel *The Brothers Karamazov* that flops on release. She stops work and puts on weight. Kennedy's presidency is generally seen as a failure, marked by the escalation of the Vietnam War, which leads to the chant 'Hey, hey, JFK, how many kids did you kill today?' President Kennedy's numerous extra-marital affairs are revealed in the media, and Jackie Kennedy leaves him.

The luck cascades on. In 1992, Bill Clinton's bid for office falters when a photo is released of him meeting Kennedy in the early 1960s. A third-party candidate, billionaire businessman Newt Sanders, wins the presidency. Monroe weds Aristotle Onassis in 1968 (and inherits his millions when he dies in 1975). In 1985, she marries astronaut Buzz Aldrin. The book's title comes from New York's main airport, which was called 'Idlewild Airport' until 1963, and would likely still bear that name if Kennedy had not been assassinated.

When I read *Idlewild*, I was tempted to write an Australian novel with a similar twist.[2] What if the build-up of plaque in Senator Bertie Milliner's coronary artery had not collapsed on 30 June 1975, but on 30 June 1977, after that year's federal election? Without Milliner's death, the numbers in the Senate would likely have allowed Gough Whitlam to pass his 1975 budget. Given time to recover from the Khemlani Loans Affair, it is imaginable that Whitlam could have won the 1977 election.

Now suppose that by 1980, rising unemployment and high inflation eventually felled the Whitlam government and led to the election of a Coalition government, with Andrew Peacock as prime minister and John Howard as treasurer. This would put Australia on the same ideological cycle as the United States (where the Republicans took over the presidency in 1980) and the United Kingdom (where the Conservatives won office in 1979).

Under a Peacock–Howard government, the economic and social reforms of the 1980s would have been among the most stringently free-market in the world. That government would have dismantled Medicare, moving Australia to a private-insurance model akin to the United States. The shift from a closed economy to an open economy might have taken place at the same time as the social safety net was shrinking. If you believe that Australia's prosperity is intertwined with our egalitarian institutions, then our economic trajectory might have been more similar to New Zealand's, whose income per person was approximately the same as Australia's a generation ago, but is now one-third smaller.

Recent decades have seen a resurgence in the field known as 'counterfactual history' – moments in which the history of the world hangs in the balance.[3] How would religious history be different if Pontius Pilate had pardoned Jesus? What if Martin Luther had become Pope rather than leading the Protestant Revolution?[4] Could a Saracen victory in France in 732 have made Islam the dominant religion in Britain today?[5] If the Spanish Armada had successfully landed in England in 1588, might the Catholic religion (not to mention the Spanish language) be dominant in the United States today?[6]

Among novelists and historians, wars are a particular focus. Some counterfactual histories are in the 'if only' category. One historian speculates that if the United States had been kept within the British Empire for another century, slavery would have been peacefully phased out, the Civil War would have been averted, and a stronger United States would have prevented the occurrence of world wars I and II.[7] Another suggests that if Mao Zedong and Zhou Enlai had asked to meet President Roosevelt in the White House, the United States might have refrained from backing the Nationalists, and the Korean and Vietnam wars might have been averted.[8]

Other counterfactuals look a good deal more troubling. Winston Churchill once wrote an essay titled 'If Lee had not won the Battle of Gettysburg' which imagines a world in which the south won the US Civil War.[9] Another historian asks what could have been if the north had won, but the south had continued to fight a guerrilla war – and concludes that the northern victors would have been forced to rule with an ever more brutal hand.[10]

World War II has inspired many counterfactuals, such as the suggestion that if the Nazis had won, the slaughter of the Jewish people might have continued in the United States.[11] The many close calls in the Cold War have also prompted counterfactuals. One historian imagines a tragedy in which the 1962 Cuban missile crisis led to Soviet submarines levelling Washington, DC, with nuclear missiles and the ensuing American retribution killing more than 100 million Russians.[12]

In Australia, historians have speculated on what would have happened if Tasmania was colonised by the French, if Alfred Deakin had issued a 'Declaration of Independence' in 1900, or if Indigenous Australians had not been assimilated.[13] Bob Hawke suggested to me that if his uncle Bert Hawke had succeeded John Curtin as federal member for Fremantle (rather than staying on in Western Australian politics, where he eventually served as premier), then Australia might have had an earlier prime minister Hawke.[14] At the heart of counterfactual history is the idea of contingency: that history is the result not only of skill and hard work, but also the dice roll of unpredictable events.

Too much commentary about politics ignores the role of chance. Political leaders are assumed to be schemers – either benevolent masterminds or Machiavellian plotters. Those who make it into parliament are regarded as having been on the trajectory to become an MP since they first became class captain. Speeches to parliament from the government imply that every policy development process is orderly. Opposition speeches often suggest that a conspiracy is at work. New opinion polls are treated with reverence, as a definitive statement of the public mood.

Yet the world is far more random than that. The very existence of each of us is stupefyingly improbable. As scientist Richard Dawkins points out, 'The potential people who could have been here in my place but who will in fact never see the light of day outnumber the sand grains of Arabia. Certainly those unborn ghosts include greater poets than Keats, scientists greater than Newton.'[15]

There is plenty of luck involved in entering politics. In my case, there are half a dozen factors which, had they gone differently, mean I would never have become a politician. When I see reporting of issues I know something about, I sometimes chuckle at the motives that are ascribed to parliamentarians on both sides of the House. In a choice between conspiracy and flub-up, choose flub-up every time.

In this book, I've attempted to weave together new stories and fresh statistics on the role of luck in Australian politics. Table 9 lists seventeen different ways that chance can affect candidates, governments, leaders and voters. These include winning top spot on the ballot (1 percentage point more of the vote for the individual candidate), rain on polling day (1.6 percentage points more of the vote for the government), and a 1 percentage point increase in the world growth rate (a 2.3 percentage point drop in the chance that the incumbent party ousts its leader).

Table 9: How luck matters

LUCKY EVENT	MAGNITUDE
LUCK FOR INDIVIDUAL CANDIDATES	
Having a parent who was a federal politician	354 times more likely to serve in federal parliament
Winning top spot on the ballot	1 percentage point more votes
Being among the most beautiful candidates	1–2 percentage points more votes
Being male	0.3 percentage points more votes
Having an Asian name	1.5 percentage points fewer votes
Having a Continental European name	0.7 percentage points fewer votes
Having a Middle Eastern name	2.3 percentage points fewer votes
Having a popular first name	0.3 percentage points more votes
Having a long surname	1.6 percentage points fewer votes
Having a hyphenated surname	2.3 percentage points fewer votes
LUCK FOR GOVERNMENTS AND OPPOSITIONS	
Rain on polling day	Government vote 1.6 percentage points higher
Hot on polling day	Government vote 1.8 percentage points lower
World economic growth 1 percentage point higher	National government 7 percentage points more likely to be re-elected
United States unemployment rate 1 percentage point higher	State governments 3–4 percentage points less likely to be re-elected
LUCK FOR LEADERS	
World economic growth 1 percentage point higher	Leader 2.3 percentage points less likely to be ousted by own party
Entry into parliament when own party is in opposition	Effect size unclear, but the last six prime ministers fit this pattern
LUCK FOR VOTERS	
Voter is male and firstborn is a son	9 percentage points more likely to vote Coalition than if firstborn was a daughter

* Beauty effect is for being among the 15% most attractive candidates. First name popularity effect is for every 1 percentage point increase in the share of the population who have that first name. Surname length effect is for having another ten characters in a person's surname. A hot polling day is one that is 10°C warmer than average for that state.

Is everything luck? Not a bit of it. In the introduction, I drew the analogy between politics and poker. Poker is a game with plenty of luck, but it also requires a good deal of skill. As it happens, I've never mastered the art of bluffing and maintaining a poker face. My poker playing is bad enough that I'd need very lucky cards indeed not to lose money.

Entrepreneur Peter Thiel uses a maths analogy to sum up the challenges that most of us face.[16] On one hand, there are *determinate* problems. Think of these as the sort of problems that can be solved with calculus – such as the trajectory of a rocket. On the other hand, there are *indeterminate* problems, which require an understanding of statistics, and thinking in terms of bell curves and uncertainty. Most of the problems we face in everyday life are indeterminate rather than determinate.

For policymakers, understanding of statistics is a great deal more useful than knowing calculus. This is partly because we are generally solving indeterminate policy problems: such as how an employment policy will reduce joblessness, how a new rail line will cut congestion, or how a climate policy will lower carbon emissions. But it's also because the political environment is itself indeterminate. Whether it's the luck of preselections, elections or the media, chance plays a central role. While it's hard to quantify the balance between luck and skill, it's tempting to conclude that, as in Machiavelli's day, luck accounts for about half of the outcomes in politics.

Some of the results I've discussed might be cute or quirky, but luck is a topic that serious people should care about. If you omit luck from your view of politics, you'll be too quick to revere the winners and revile the losers. Putting chance back into the picture allows for a more balanced perspective on politics, and a reminder of the myriad ways that luck shapes all our lives.

Acknowledging the role of chance in politics ensures that its practitioners can learn from failure just as entrepreneurs do. To over-punish luck is to risk missing out on the insights of those, like Lincoln and Churchill, who suffered early setbacks. Conversely, ignoring luck may mean paying too much attention to old-school campaigners and pollsters – whose approaches have all the merit of water diviners and palm readers.

In an age of hyperpartisanship, luck matters more than ever before. As parties move apart, the effect of luck isn't merely to move someone between the moderate left and the moderate right; it's the difference between extremes. Chance raises the stakes for serious reformers, but our job is no less important than it's ever been.

Wish us luck.

ACKNOWLEDGEMENTS

When I interviewed him for this book, Bob Hawke said that his luck began with the fact that his family 'was always extremely loving, but they also gave me a feeling of confidence'.[1] I had similarly good fortune. I was born in the year when Gough Whitlam won office, and my mother reportedly pinned an 'It's Time' badge on her nine-month belly. Ours was a household with a sense of both social justice and curiosity. Plenty of the anecdotes in this book – such as the 1961 election being decided on Communist Party preferences – were stories I first learned about in conversations with my parents Barbara and Michael and my brother Tim.

This book draws on various of my own academic papers, including co-authored research with Alison Booth, Paul Burke, Joshua Gans, Amy King, Mark McLeish, Phillip Metaxas, Tirta Susilo, Elena Varganova and Justin Wolfers. My thanks to each of those collaborators for all I learned from them, as well as to the referees and journal editors who improved our work through the publication process.

I've enjoyed many conversations about luck with parliamentary colleagues, journalists, academics and the engaged electors of Fraser. Particular thanks to Dennis Altman, Tony Atkinson, Gai Brodtmann, Mal Brough, Bob Carr, Julie Collins, Phillip Coorey, Annabel Crabb, Sam Dastyari, Andrew Egan, Bob Ellis, Kate Ellis, Joel Fitzgibbon, Peter FitzSimons, Kieran Gilbert, Dennis Glover, Antony Green, Peter Hartcher, Bob Hawke, Joanna Heath, Phil Hore, John Howard, Fran Kelly, Paul Kelly, Brad Manera, Thomas McMahon, George Megalogenis, Laurie Oakes, Brendan Pearson, Nova Peris, John Quiggin, Michelle Rowland, Joanne Ryan, Leigh Sales, Amelia Simpson, Ed Smith, Lenore Taylor, Laura Tingle, Lyndell Tutty and Christine Wallace. I'm especially indebted to Terri Butler, Nick Champion, Jason Clare, Barbara Leigh, Jennifer Rayner and Nick Terrell for taking the time to read early drafts and provide valuable feedback.

In locating stories and crunching statistics, I've been fortunate to have the assistance of a bevy of researchers, including Cameron Amos, Caitlin Bunker, Harry Dalton, Alexandra Downie, Lillian Hannock, Kieran Heid, Matthew Jacob, Luke Martin, Ben Molan, Griffen Murphy, Michael Quincey O'Neill, Tom Russell-Penny, Joseph Walker, Matthew Woodroffe and John Zerilli.

For a writer, there is nothing so auspicious as an erudite editor. My thanks to Chris Feik and his talented team at Black Inc., including cover designer Peter Long, copy-editor Kirstie Innes-Will and publicist Jessica Pearce.

Since parts of this book use the Household, Income and Labour Dynamics in Australia survey, I am required to acknowledge that this survey was initiated and is funded by the Australian Government Department of Social Services, and is managed by the Melbourne Institute of Applied Economic and

Social Research. My findings and views based on these data should not be attributed to either body. My analysis also draws in part on various datasets held with the Australian Data Archive.

Because I think differently when I'm exercising, this is surely a better book thanks to the staff who maintain the Parliament House gym, Dickson pool and Civic pool, as well as the many kangaroos I've chanced to encounter while running around Lake Burley Griffin, Mount Ainslie and Mount Majura.

Meeting my wife Gweneth was the luckiest thing that ever happened to me, and I feel fortunate each day to have an idealistic partner who helps me keep politics in perspective. If the results in Chapter 2 are correct, my three sons, Sebastian, Theodore and Zachary, might have nudged me to the right. To my remarkable boys: I forgive you for this, and hope you'll forgive me in turn for the hours spent researching and writing this book in evenings and on weekends. May the chances in life come your way, and may you seize them when they do.

ENDNOTES

1 Why Politics is More Like Poker than Chess

1   My account of the 1940 air disaster draws on the excellent work of Cameron Hazlehurst, 2013, *Ten Journeys to Cameron's Farm: An Australian tragedy*, ANU E-Press, Canberra.

2   Wilfred Compagnoni, quoted in Hazlehurst, 2013, p. 92.

3   Desmond Woods, 2010, 'La Perouse: Where fate beckons [Book Review]', *Headmark: Journal of the Australian Naval Institute*, 136: 64–6.

4   Joëlle Gergis, David J. Karoly and Robert J. Allan, 2009, 'A climate reconstruction of Sydney Cove, New South Wales, using weather journal and documentary data, 1788–1791', *Australian Meteorological and Oceanographic Journal*, 53(2): 83–98; Joëlle Gergis, Don Garden and Claire Fenby, 2010, 'The influence of climate on the first European settlement of Australia: A comparison of weather journals, documentary data and palaeoclimate records, 1788–1793', *Environmental History*, 15(3): 485–507.

5   'Terrible plane disaster', *Kalgoorlie Miner*, 14 August 1940, p. 4.

6   Andy McSmith, 1996, *Faces of Labour: The inside story*, Verso, London, p. 34. In the 1983 election, both Cherie Blair (then Cherie Booth) and Tony Blair ran as Labour candidates. There was a good deal of luck in the fact that she won preselection for in a strong Conservative area, while he won preselection in a strong Labour area.

7   Benjamin F. Jones and Benjamin A. Olken, 2009. 'Hit or Miss? The effect of assassinations on institutions and war', *American Economic Journal: Macroeconomics*, 1(2): 55–87.

8   For other examples, see Bob Ellis, 1997, *Goodbye Jerusalem: Night thoughts of a Labor outsider*, Vintage, Sydney, p. 26.

9   Patricia O'Toole, 'The speech that saved Teddy Roosevelt's life', *Smithsonian Magazine*, November 2012.

10   Craig Whitney, 'I.R.A. attacks 10 Downing Street with mortar fire as Cabinet meets', *The New York Times*, 8 February 1991.

11   Hazlehurst, 2013, pp. 541–50.

12   Robert Menzies, 1967, *Afternoon Light: Some memories of men and events*, Cassell, London, p. 18.

13   Hazlehurst, 2013, pp. 620–3.

14   Hazlehurst, 2013, pp. 619–20.

15   The 10,000 hour rule originated in K. Anders Ericsson, Michael J. Prietula and Edward T. Cokely, 'The making of an expert', *Harvard Business Review*, July–August 2007. The rule was popularised by Malcolm Gladwell, 2008, *Outliers: The story of success*, Little, Brown and Company, New York, pp. 39–42. For a critique of Gladwell's interpretation of the rule, see David Bradley, 2012, *Deceived Wisdom: Why what you thought was right is wrong*, Elliott & Thompson, London, pp. 101–4.

16   In chapter 25 of *The Prince* (1513), Machiavelli writes: 'It is not unknown to me how many men have had, and still have, the opinion that the affairs of the world are in such wise governed by fortune and by God that men with their wisdom cannot direct them and that no one can even help them; and because of this they would have us believe that it is not necessary to labour much in affairs, but to let chance govern them. This opinion has been more credited in our times because of the great changes in affairs which have been seen, and may still be seen, every day, beyond all human conjecture. Sometimes pondering over this, I am in some degree inclined to their opinion. Nevertheless, not to extinguish our free will, I hold it to be true that Fortune is the arbiter of one-half of our actions, but that she still leaves us to direct the other half, or perhaps a little less.'

17   For an engaging account of Piff's research, see Lisa Miller, 'The money-empathy gap', *New York Magazine*, 1 July 2012.

18   This quote is generally attributed to US football coach Barry Switzer.

19   For an excellent discussion of the relationship between luck and inequality, see Christopher Jencks, 1972, *Inequality: A reassessment of the effect of family and schooling in America*, Basic Books, New York.

2 What is Luck?

1   See Microsoft Support, 2011, 'Description of the RAND function in Excel', Article ID: 828795 and Microsoft Developer Network, 2008, 'Randomize Function (Visual Basic)' (help page).

2   Subsequent developments in quantum mechanics have cast some doubt on Laplace's Demon. Moreover, computing estimates show that it would be impossible to construct a computer that would process all of the information held in the universe.

3   Paul Demont ('Allotment and democracy in Ancient Greece', published in booksandideas.net, 13 December 2010) summarises the situation as follows: 'In the Constitution of Athens, the description "chosen by lot" thus turns up again and again in the second part of the treatise, for "all the ordinary offices" (ch. 43, 1), with the exception of the treasurers of military and public entertainment funds, the superintendent of the springs, and for military functions in general. Let us count the offices chosen by lot: 500 bouleutai, 10 treasurers of Athena, 10 sellers, 10 tax collectors, 10 accountants, 10 verifiers (along with 2 assessors), 1 steward, 10 guardians of the temples, 10 officials in charge of the city, 10 in charge of the markets, 10 surveyors of measures, 10 then 35 wheat guards, 10 supervisors of the port, the Eleven, 5 initiators of legal proceedings in eisagogè, 40 for other kinds of proceedings, 5 roadway officials, 10 accountants (and 10 associates), 1 secretary of the prytanium (formerly elected), a secretary of the laws, 10 sacrificers, 10 superintendents of feasts, 1 archon of Salamis, 1 demarch of the Piraeus, 9 archons and their secretary to draw lots for judges, 10 organizers of Dionysia, and 10 in charge of contests. Thus in total several hundreds of officeholders chosen by lot each year, who in each

cohort could not be renewed (with rare exceptions), to which must be added the 6,000 heliasts already mentioned, who were themselves subject to reselection by lot day after day, between tribunals.'

4   One estimate suggests that half of Athenians would have had the chance to serve as leader: Christopher W. Blackwell, 'Athenian democracy: An overview,' in C. Blackwell (ed.), *Dēmos: Classical Athenian Democracy* (*The Stoa: A consortium for electronic publication in the humanities*, A. A. Mahoney and R. Scaife (eds)), p. 24. However, I have used a more conservative estimate of the number of citizens (closer to 40,000 than 20,000), which puts the share closer to one-quarter.

5   Nicholas Rescher, *Luck: The brilliant randomness of everyday life*, Farrar, Straus Giroux, New York, 1995, p. 6.

6   Rescher, 1995, p. 137.

7   Thomas Nagel, *Mortal Questions*, Cambridge University Press, Cambridge, 1979, pp. 24–38. Nagel also includes a fourth category – causal luck – but subsequent scholars have argued that this fits within the existing categories of circumstantial and resultant luck.

8   The examples in this paragraph are drawn from: David Epstein, *The Sports Gene: Inside the science of extraordinary performance*, Penguin, New York, 2013; David Epstein, 'Are athletes really getting faster, better, stronger?', TED Talk, March 2014.

9   This story is mentioned in Rescher, 1995, p. 86.

10   The examples in this paragraph are taken from Richard Gaughan, *Accidental Genius: The world's greatest by-chance discoveries*, Thomas Allen, Markham, Ontario, 2012; Andrew Boyd, 'Serendipity and the inventive mind', *The Engines of Our Ingenuity*, Episode 2463, Houston Public Radio, 2009.

11   Guy Faguet, 2008, *The War on Cancer: An anatomy of failure, a blueprint for the future*, Springer, Dordrecht, The Netherlands, p. 66.

12   The examples in this paragraph are drawn from William Ogburn and Dorothy Thomas, 1922, 'Are inventions inevitable? A note on social evolution', *Political Science Quarterly*, 37(1): 83–98; David Lamb and Susan Easton, 1984, *Multiple Discovery: The pattern of scientific progress*,

Avebury, Buckinghamshire; Malcolm Gladwell, 'Who says big ideas are rare?', *The New Yorker*, 12 May 2008.

13   Rescher, 1995, p. 20.

14   David Marr, 2014, 'The Century of Archduke Ferdinand's Assassination', *The Saturday Paper*, 28 June, p. 7.

15   Ed Smith, 2012, *Luck: What it means and why it matters*, Bloomsbury, London, p. 163.

16   David Johnson, *The Man Who Didn't Shoot Hitler: The story of Henry Tandey VC and Adolf Hitler, 1918*, History Press, London, 2013.

17   Rescher, 1995, p. 3.

18   A 1945 US military memorandum that set out options for nuclear targets estimated the population of Kokura at 178,000 and Nagasaki at 210,000, making the bombed city nearly one-fifth larger than the initial target.

19   The examples in this paragraph are drawn from Louis Menand, 'Nukes of Hazard', *The New Yorker*, 30 September 2013, pp. 76–80 (a review of Eric Schlosser, *Command and Control: Nuclear weapons, the Damascus accident, and the illusion of safety*, Penguin, New York, 2013).

20   Erich Remarque (translated by Virginia Wurdak), *All Quiet on the Western Front*, Continuum, New York, 2004 [1929], p. 53.

21   Email from Brad Manera to author, 7 May 2015.

22   C.J. Chivers, 'Foot on bomb, marine defies a Taliban trap', *The New York Times*, 23 January 2010, p. A1.

23   Two excellent accounts of the torpedo episode on 12 July 1940 are: Roger Averill, 2012, *Exile: The lives and hopes of Werner Pelz*, Melbourne, Transit Lounge, chapter 5 [e-book without page numbers]; Helen Fry, *From Dachau to D-Day: The refugee who fought for Britain*, The History Press, Stroud, Gloucestershire, 2011, chapter 4 [e-book without page numbers].

24   The stories of the *Dunera* boys are set out in Ken Inglis, 2010, 'From Berlin to the bush', *The Monthly*, 59: 48–53.

25   I am grateful to Bruce Chapman, whose speech at the unveiling of Fred Gruen's portrait on 6 May 2014 discussed the chance role of the torpedo (and paid tribute to the 'unknown incompetent German torpedo-checker who kept Fred Gruen alive').

26   James Feyrer and Bruce Sacerdote, 2009, 'Colonialism and modern income: Islands as natural experiments', *Review of Economics and Statistics*, 91(2): 245–62.

27   Daron Acemoglu, Simon Johnson and James Robinson, 2010, 'The colonial origins of comparative development: An empirical investigation', *American Economic Review*, 91(5): 1369–401.

28   C. Justin Cook, 2014, 'The role of lactase persistence in pre-colonial development', *Journal of Economic Growth*, 19(4): 369–406.

29   Jared Diamond, 1997, *Guns, Germs, and Steel: The fates of human societies*, W.W. Norton, New York.

30   Jared Diamond, 2013, 'How geography creates history', *Pop Up Ideas*, BBC Radio 4, 25 December; Jared Diamond, 1998, 'Japanese roots', *Discover Magazine*, June.

31   Ian McLean, 2013, *Why Australia Prospered: The shifting sources of economic growth*, Princeton University Press, Princeton, p. 87.

32   Among the possible reasons for the small claim size were that (a) significant numbers of men had already arrived at the goldfields, and larger claim sizes would have created a policing challenge as they were turned away; (b) Victoria simply followed New South Wales, which had set small claim sizes for its goldfields; (c) the combination of high licence fees and small claim sizes maximised government revenue; and (d) larger areas were harder for claimants to monitor, which might have led to more cheating, and perhaps law and order challenges. See Sumner J. La Croix, 1992, 'Property rights and institutional change during Australia's gold rush', *Explorations in Economic History*, 29(2): 204–227. Ironically – given the government's concern about law and order problems – the high licence fees and small claim sizes led to the 1854 Eureka Rebellion.

33   Daron Acemoglu and James Robinson, 2013, 'Economics versus politics: Pitfalls of policy advice', *Journal of Economic Perspectives*, 27(2): 173–92.

34   McLean, 2013, pp. 63–7, 96–100.

35   Geoffrey Blainey, 1982, *A Land Half Won* (revised edition), Macmillan, Melbourne, p. 201, cited in Ian McLean, 2013, p. 135.

36   David Gruen, 2011, 'The macroeconomic and structural implications of a once-in-a-lifetime boom in the terms of trade', Speech to Australian Business Economists, 24 November 2011. Another example of the impact of luck on economic performance is given by William Easterly, who experiments with randomly assigning 125 countries annual growth rates varying between –2 and 6 per cent. After forty years, the best-performing country has twice the income of the worst performer. See William Easterly, 2002, *The Elusive Quest for Growth: Economists' adventures and misadventures in the tropics*, MIT Press, Cambridge, MA, pp. 212–13.

37   The chart is adjusted to account for fact that there are more parliamentary debates in some years than others. In the absence of an authoritative count of words spoken in parliament each year, I instead normalise by dividing by the total number of times each year the words 'Monday', 'Tuesday' and 'Wednesday' are mentioned. Results are similar when using other common words as a divisor.

38   Matthew Syed, 2011, *Bounce: The myth of talent and the power of practice*, Fourth Estate, London; Smith, 2012, pp. 11–13.

39   Helene Cooper, 2012, 'A bit of quiet optimism, and some superstition, before a tight victory', *The New York Times*, 6 November.

40   Brian Loughnane, 2013, 'Brian Loughnane's diary', *The Spectator Australia*, 21 September.

3 Political Parents, Sliding Doors and the Daughter Effect

1   Author's interview with John Howard, 5 December 2014.

2   Quoted in Graham Freudenberg, 2011, 'Gough Whitlam and NSW Labor', *Voice*, 30 November 2011.

3   Mark Latham, 2005, *The Latham Diaries*, Melbourne University Press, Melbourne, p. 25.

4   For a thorough account of the preselection, see Terry Giesecke, 2012, 'Preselection 2010: The ALP selects its candidate for Fraser', *Australian Policy Online*, 20 February.

5   Michael Gordon, 1993, *Paul Keating: A question of leadership*, University of Queensland Press, Brisbane, p. 40; Ray Gietzelt, 2004, *Worth Fighting For: The memoirs of Ray Gietzelt, General Secretary of the Federated Miscellaneous Workers Union of Australia, 1955-1984*, Federation Press, Sydney, p. 102.

6   Accounts of the Whitlam result vary. I use Whitlam 249 to Mallam 169, which is drawn from a newspaper account a few days later: 'Werriwa Labour Pre-selection', *The Biz*, 24 April 1952, p. 10, available at <http://nla.gov.au/nla.news-article75594974>.

7   Amy King and Andrew Leigh, 2009, 'Bias at the ballot box: Testing whether candidates' gender affects their vote', CEPR Discussion Paper 625, Australian National University, Canberra, Appendix Table 2 (which shows 1349 preselection applicants for 219 major party candidate positions).

8   In the House of Representatives for the 2013 election, women made up 49 out of 150 Labor candidates, and 34 out of 160 candidates for the Coalition parties (the Liberal Party, National Party, Liberal National Party and Country Liberal Party). The Coalition parties ran more candidates (160) than electorates (150) because their agreement allows three-cornered contests in open seats.

9   Amy King and Andrew Leigh, 2009, Appendix tables 3 and 4. (This detail does not appear in the published version: Amy King and Andrew Leigh, 2010, 'Bias at the ballot box? Testing whether candidates' gender affects their vote,' *Social Science Quarterly*, 91:2, pp. 324–43.

10   For an analysis, see King and Leigh, 2010, pp. 324–43.

11   The number of people eligible to stand for parliament since 1901 is calculated as 29 million, being the sum of the adult population in 1901, plus births from 1880–1995 (minus infant deaths over that period), plus permanent arrivals from 1901–2010. Naturally, this is only an approximation. For example, it ignores emigration by children, and includes some permanent migrants who do not take up citizenship. Data on political dynasties were provided by Martin Lumb.

His dataset includes thirty federal parliamentarians with a parent in federal politics, and 120 with some other kind of family connection (such as parent, grandparent, grandchild, cousin or sibling).

12 These figures are calculated from the unconfidentialised version of the 2006 HILDA survey (and were crunched in a secure data environment during my time at the Australian National University).

13 Limiting the sample to occupations with more than 15 respondents, none of the 336 occupations in the HILDA sample has a higher dynastic bias than federal politics.

14 The US estimate of dynastic bias is from Ernesto Dal Bó, Pedro Dal Bó and Jason Snyder, 2009, 'Political dynasties', *Review of Economic Studies*, 76(1): 115–42. As they admit, their estimate that 1 in 10,000 Americans ever serve in Congress is likely to be biased upwards. To see this, note that I estimate that 1 in 17,000 Australians ever serve in federal parliament. At a single point in time, the share of the population serving in federal parliament is 1 in 600,000 in the US, and 1 in 100,000 in Australia.

15 Bob Hawke, quoted in Paul Kelly, 1992, *The End of Certainty: The story of the 1980s*, Allen & Unwin, Sydney, p. 141.

16 Annabel Crabb, 2014, 'Sisterhood salutes all those daddy's girls', *The Canberra Times*, 9 March, p. 2.

17 Henrietta Cook, 2013, 'How life with Jack opened a premier's eyes', *The Age*, 8 June.

18 Tony Abbott, 'Address to the International Women's Day Parliamentary Breakfast', Parliament House, Canberra, 4 March 2014.

19 Analysis is based on publicly available information on the children of MPs and senators in the forty-fourth parliament (based on Senate composition before July 2014), and covers 199 out of 226 parliamentarians. The analysis focuses on the total number of children rather than the first-born child since it is difficult to discern from publicly available data the sex of the first child.

20 Another clear pattern is that male parliamentarians have, on average, one more child than their female counterparts. For a discussion of this difference, see Annabel Crabb, 2014, *The Wife Drought*, Random House, Sydney.

21   Ebonya Washington, 'Female socialization: How daughters affect their
      legislator fathers' voting on women's issues', *American Economic Review*,
      2008, 98(1): 311–32.

22   Of the parliamentarians in my 2013 sample, forty-two were men who
      were in parliament when the 2006 conscience vote on abortifacient
      drug RU-486 took place. Unlike Ebonya Washington's study of US
      legislators, I do not find any statistically significant association between
      how male parliamentarians voted on RU-486 and the gender of their
      children. However, a proper analysis of the issue would require coding
      the gender of all parliamentarians who participated in the vote, not
      merely those who remained in the parliament seven years later. Due to
      the difficulty of obtaining data on retired parliamentarians' children, I
      did not carry out such an analysis.

23   Michael S. Dahl, Cristian L. Dezsö and David Gaddis Ross, 2012,
      'Fatherhood and managerial style: How a male CEO's children affect
      the wages of his employees', *Administrative Science Quarterly*, 57(4):
      669–93; Adam Glynn and Maya Sen, 2015, 'Identifying judicial
      empathy: Does having daughters cause judges to rule for women's
      issues?' *American Journal of Political Science*, 59(1): 37–54.

24   Philip G. Zimbardo, 2007, 'Revisiting the Stanford Prison Experiment:
      A lesson in the power of situation', *Chronicle of Higher Education*,
      53(30): B6. Zimbardo argues that situational effects explain many
      phenomena, from the prison abuses at Abu Ghraib to the mass suicide
      of 919 followers of Reverend Jim Jones in Guyana. See also Philip G.
      Zimbardo, 2007, *The Lucifer Effect: Understanding how good people turn
      evil*, Random House, New York.

4 Donkey Voting, Beauty and Unusual Names

1   Charles McGrath, quoted in 'The Ballarat Seat', 1920, *Daily Telegraph*
      (Launceston), 6 January, p. 6, available at <http://nla.gov.au/nla.news-
      article152904620>.

2   Antony Green, 2013, 'WA Senate contest comes down to just 1 vote –
      and it's one of the missing', Antony Green's Election Blog, 8 November;
      Antony Green, 2014, 'WA Senate re-election – What happens next?',

20 February 2014 (both available at <http://blogs.abc.net.au/ antonygreen/>). See also Australian Electoral Commission, 2013, 'AEC releases voting preference information recorded for WA missing votes', Media Release, 8 November.

3   So did Electoral Commissioner Ed Killesteyn, who resigned after his organisation could not explain how the 1370 ballots had been lost.

4   For a good profile of Glenn Druery, see Tony Walker, 2014, 'The vote peddler', *Australian Financial Review*, 27 December, p. 17.

5   F.R. Beasley, 1952, 'The parliament of the commonwealth', in R. Else-Mitchell (ed.) *Essays on the Australian Constitution*, Law Book Co., Sydney, p. 62, quoted in Murray Goot, 1985, 'Electoral systems', in Don Aitken (ed.), *Surveys of Australian Political Science*, Allen & Unwin, Sydney, pp. 179–264.

6   D.M. Davies, 1939, *How Australia is Governed. A programme of safeguards for Australian democracy*, The Council for Civil Liberties, Melbourne, p. 22, quoted in Goot, 1985, pp. 179–264.

7   Goot, 1985, pp. 179–264.

8   Mungo MacCallum, *Mungo: The man who laughs*, Duffy & Snellgrove, Sydney, 2001, pp. 64–5.

9   Malcolm Mackerras, 1970, 'Preference voting and the "donkey vote"', *Politics*, 5(1): 69–76.

10   Amy King and Andrew Leigh, 2009, 'Are ballot order effects heterogeneous?' *Social Science Quarterly*, 90(1): 71–87.

11   Mackerras, 1970: 69–76.

12   The 1996 and 1998 results are found in King and Leigh, 2009.

13   Our study coded more than 15,000 candidates who have run for office, and held constant factors that might affect the result, such as the candidate's party, the number of other people on the ballot, and the vote that a candidate of that party would expect to receive in that electorate.

14   In the US, female incumbents in House elections over the period 1984–1992 received a 6 percentage-point higher vote share than male incumbents: Jeffrey Milyo and Samantha Schosberg, 2000, 'Gender

bias and selection bias in House elections,' *Public Choice*, 105: 41–59. Our study found a gender penalty of around 5 percentage points in the 1940s and 1950s, falling to about one-third of a percentage point from 1980 to 2004: King and Leigh, 2010.

15   This was the campaign slogan of Anna Belle Clement O'Brien when she ran for the Tennessee state senate in 1976.

16   T. Besley and A. Case, 2000, 'Unnatural experiments? Estimating the incidence of endogenous policies', *Economic Journal*, 110(467); T. Besley and A. Case, 2002, 'Political institutions and policy choices: Evidence from the United States', *Journal of Economic Literature*, 41(1); A. Case, 1998, 'The effects of stronger child support enforcement of non-marital fertility' in Irwin Garfinkel, Sara McLanahan, Daniel Meyer and Judith Seltzer (eds) *Fathers Under Fire: The revolution in child support enforcement*, Russell Sage Foundation.

17   Andrew Leigh, 2005, 'Economic voting and electoral behavior: How do individual, local and national factors affect the partisan choice?' *Economics and Politics*, 17(2): 265–96.

18   For Australian trends, see, for example, an analysis based on Newspoll data: Peter Brent, 2011, 'Abbott the bloke magnet', *Mumble Politics*, 28 September, <http://blogs.theaustralian.news.com.au/mumble/index.php/theaustralian/comments/newspoll_september_2011_quarterly>. For European evidence, see Lena Edlund, Rohini Pande and Laila Haider, 2005, 'Unmarried parenthood and redistributive politics', *Journal of the European Economic Association*, 3(1): 95–119. For US evidence, see Lena Edlund and Rohini Pande, 2002, 'Why have women become left-wing: The political gender gap and the decline in marriage', *Quarterly Journal of Economics*, 117: 917–61.

19   The Australian literature on parliamentarians' ethnicity is surprisingly thin. For an exception, see Gianni Zappala, 1998,'The influence of the ethnic composition of Australian federal electorates on the parliamentary responsiveness of MPs to their ethnic sub-constituencies', *Australian Journal of Political Science*, 33(2): 187–209.

20   The effects for Muslim names are statistically significant at the 10 per cent level, for Continental European names at the 11 per cent level, and for Asian names at the 19 per cent level. Effects for Jewish, Hispanic

and African names are not statistically significant at conventional levels. Interestingly, OnoMAP codes founding father King O'Malley as being of Asian ethnicity. Omitting him from the sample makes little difference to the estimates.

21   Alison Booth, Andrew Leigh and Elena Varganova, 2012, 'Does racial and ethnic discrimination vary across minority groups? Evidence from a field experiment', *Oxford Bulletin of Economics and Statistics*, 74(4): 547–73.

22   Bill O'Chee, quoted in Gabrielle Chan, 1996, 'O'Chee urges Hanson to halt violence', *The Australian*, 31 October, p. 6.

23   Andrew Leigh and Tirta Susilo, 2009, 'Is voting skin-deep? Estimating the effect of candidate ballot photographs on election outcomes', *Journal of Economic Psychology*, 30(1): 61–70.

24   NT election: John Taylor, 'Aboriginal candidate withdraws', *ABC AM*, 14 August 2001.

25   Average US height data from M.A. McDowell, C.D. Fryar, C.L. Ogden, K.M. Flegal, 2008, 'Anthropometric reference data for children and adults: United States, 2003–2006', National health statistics reports, no 10. National Center for Health Statistics, Hyattsville, MD.

26   Nicola Persico, Andrew Postlewaite and Dan Silverman, 2004, 'The effect of adolescent experience on labor market outcomes: The case of height', *Journal of Political Economy*, 112(5): 1019–53.

27   Jacqueline Kent, 2010, *The Making of Julia Gillard*, Penguin, Melbourne.

28   Amy King and Andrew Leigh, 2009, 'Beautiful politicians', *Kyklos*, 62(4): 579–93.

29   This turns out to be a common finding in the literature. See, for example, the survey by Judith H. Langlois, Lisa Kalakanis, Adam J. Rubenstein, Andrea Larson, Monica Hallam and Monica Smoot, 2000, 'Maxims or myths of beauty? A meta-analytic and theoretical review', *Psychological Bulletin*, 126(3): 390–423.

30   Judith H. Langlois, Lori A. Roggman, Rita J. Casey, Jean M. Ritter, Loretta A. Rieser-Danner and Vivian Y. Jenkins, 1987, 'Infant preferences for attractive faces: Rudiments of a stereotype?' *Developmental Psychology*, 23(3): 363.

31 Misha Schubert, 2006, 'Pretty plain that we prefer our pollies to be crackers', *The Age*, 6 December.

32 Andrew Bolt, 2006, 'ANU's next big survey: What the bloke at the bar told me', 10 December, <http://blogs.news.com.au/heraldsun/andrewbolt/index.php/heraldsun/comments/anus_next_big_survey_what_the_bloke_at_the_bar_told_me/>.

33 M. Klein and U. Rosar, 2005. 'Physische Attraktivität und Wahlerfolg. Eine empirische Analyse am Beispiel der Wahlkreiskandidaten bei der Bundestagswahl 2002', *Politische Vierteljahresschrift*, 46(2): 266–90; Niclas Berggren, Henrik Jordahl and Panu Poutvaara, 2010, 'The looks of a winner: Beauty and electoral success', *Journal of Public Economics*, 94(1): 8–15. Another paper finds that beauty matters even between contenders for national office: Harry Garretsen, Janka Stoker, Rob J.M. Alessie and Joris Lammers, 2014, 'Simply a matter of luck and looks? Predicting elections when both the world economy and the psychology of faces count', CESifo Working Paper 4857, CESifo, Munich.

34 C.E. Landry, J.A. List, M.K. Price and N.G. Rupp, 2006, 'Toward an understanding of the Economics of Charity: Evidence from a field experiment', *Quarterly Journal of Economics*, 121(6): 747–82; M. Belot, V. Bhaskar & J. van de Ven, 2012, 'Beauty and the sources of discrimination', *Journal of Human Resources*, 47: 851–72; N. Mocan & E. Tekin, 2010, 'Ugly criminals', *Review of Economics and Statistics*, 92: 15–30.

35 Ronald Mazzella and Alan Feingold, 1994, 'The effects of physical attractiveness, race, socioeconomic status, and gender of defendants and victims on judgments of mock jurors: A meta-analysis', *Journal of Applied Social Psychology*, 24(15): 1315–38; John E. Stewart, 1980, 'Defendant's attractiveness as a factor in the outcome of criminal trials: An observational study', *Journal of Applied Social Psychology*, 10(4): 348–61.

36 J.R. Nethercote, 'Unearthing the Seven Dwarfs and the Age of the Mandarins', Obituaries Australia, National Centre of Biography, Australian National University, <http://adb.anu.edu.au/essay/5/text26981>, originally published 5 October 2012, accessed 19 December 2014.

37 Yariv Tsfati, Dana Markowitz Elfassi and Israel Waismel-Manor, 2010, 'Exploring the association between Israeli legislators' physical attractiveness and their television news coverage', *The International Journal of Press/Politics*, 15: 175–92.

38 Yusaku Horiuchi, Tadashi Komatsu and Fumio Nakaya, 2012, 'Should candidates smile to win elections? An application of automated face recognition technology', Crawford School Research Paper No. 2, Australian National University.

39 Daniel Hamermesh, 2011, *Beauty Pays: Why attractive people are more successful*, Princeton University Press, Princeton, N.J.

40 Leif D. Nelson and Joseph P. Simmons, 2007, 'Moniker maladies: When names sabotage success', *Psychological Science*, 18(12): 1106–12.

41 Brett W. Pelham, Matthew C. Mirenberg and John T. Jones, 2002, 'Why Susie sells seashells by the seashore: Implicit egotism and major life decisions', *Journal of Personality and Social Psychology*, 82(4): 469–87.

42 Ernest L. Abel and Michael L. Kruger, 2009, 'Athletes, doctors, and lawyers with first names beginning with 'D' die sooner.' *Death Studies*, 34(1): 71–81. But see also a rebuttal paper: Gary Smith, 2012, 'Do people whose names begin with "D" really die young?' *Death Studies*, 36(2): 182–89.

43 John T. Jones, Brett W. Pelham, Matthew C. Mirenberg and John J. Hetts, 2002, 'Name letter preferences are not merely mere exposure: Implicit egotism as self-regulation', *Journal of Experimental Social Psychology*, 38(2): 170–7.

44 Nelson and Simmons, 2007: 1106–12.

45 Stephanie Rosenbloom, 2008, 'Names that match forge a bond on the internet', *The New York Times*, 10 April.

46 Randy Gamer, 2005, 'What's in a name? Persuasion perhaps', *Journal of Consumer Psychology*, 15(2): 108–16.

47 Jeremy Bailenson, quoted in Rosenbloom, 2008.

48 Alexandra Alter, 'The baby-name business', *Wall Street Journal*, 22 June 2007, p. W1.

49   The total number of NSW births is derived from Australian Bureau of
     Statistics, 2014, *Australian Historical Population Statistics, 2014*, Cat.
     No. 3105.0.65.001, ABS, Canberra, Table 4.1.

50   Formally, I carry out two-sample tests of proportion, and report those
     first names for which the difference is statistically significant at the
     5 per cent level.

51   This analysis uses a name database provided by the New South Wales
     Register of Births, Deaths and Marriages, covering all names given to
     ten or more babies in each year from 1952 to 2008. The dataset covers
     about four million of the five million babies born in New South Wales
     over that period. My empirical analysis holds constant the election, the
     candidate's gender and the candidate's party.

52   David E. Kalist and Daniel Y. Lee, 2009, 'First names and crime: Does
     unpopularity spell trouble?' *Social Science Quarterly*, 90(1): 39–49. The
     data is drawn from a large US state (which the authors do not identify
     for reasons for confidentiality). Note that this is not merely a racial
     effect – the pattern holds when black people and white people are
     analysed separately.

53   Admittedly, these two categories are not mutually exclusive.

54   The average length of senators' surnames is 6.8 characters. The average
     length of MPs' surnames is 6.5 characters. Most of this difference in
     surname length is due to the three senators with hyphenated surnames
     (Fierravanti-Wells, Hanson-Young and Whish-Wilson).

55   Daniel Müller and Lionel Page, 2013, 'Political selection and the relative
     age effect', Working Paper, Queensland University of Technology.
     Using political birthdate data supplied by Philip Clarke, and school
     entry cutoffs listed in Andrew Leigh and Chris Ryan, 2008, 'Estimating
     returns to education using different natural experiment techniques',
     Economics of Education Review, 27(2): 149–60, I checked for similar
     effects in Australia, but did not observe any such pattern. On Australian
     sports stars' birthdays, see Andrew Leigh, 2014, *The Economics of Just
     About Everything*, Allen & Unwin, Sydney, pp. 58–61.

5 Weather, Sharks and the World Economy

1   Christopher H. Achen and Larry M. Bartels. 2013, 'Blind Retrospection: Why shark attacks are bad for democracy', Center for the Study of Democratic Institutions, Vanderbilt University, Working Paper 5-2013.

2   Achen and Bartels, 2013.

3   Jared M. Diamond, 2005, *Collapse: How societies choose to fail or succeed*, Viking, New York, NY, p. 168.

4   Achen and Bartels, 2013.

5   Emily Oster, 2004, 'Witchcraft, weather and economic growth in renaissance Europe.' *Journal of Economic Perspectives*, 18(1): 215–28.

6   Edward Miguel, 2005, 'Poverty and witch killing.' *Review of Economic Studies*, 72(4): 1153–72.

7   C. Hovland and R. Sears, 1940, 'Minor studies of aggression: Correlation of lynchings with economic indices', *Journal of Psychology*, 9: 301–10; Joseph Hepworth and Stephen West, 1988, 'Lynchings and the economy: A time-series reanalysis of Hovland and Sears (1940)', *Journal of Personality and Social Psychology*, 55(2): 239–47; but cf Donald Green, Jack Glaser and A. Rich, 1998, 'From lynching to gay-bashing: The elusive connection between economic conditions and hate crime', *Journal of Personality and Social Psychology*, 75(1): 82–92.

8   Paul Burke and Andrew Leigh, 2010, 'Do output contractions trigger democratic change?' *American Economic Journal: Macroeconomics 2*, 4: 124–57.

9   A study using panel data for 156 countries from 1975 to 2010 concludes that a one standard deviation increase in the occurrence of floods, extreme temperatures, earthquakes and windstorms increases the likelihood that a government is replaced by 0.62, 0.34, 0.21 and 0.46 percentage points, respectively. The effect is stronger in non-OECD countries (which are more likely to be non-democracies). See Chun-Ping Chang and Aziz N. Berdiev, 2015, 'Do natural disasters increase the likelihood that a government is replaced?' *Applied Economics*, 47(17): 1788–1808.

10   Specifically, I regress the two-party vote in a state or territory on data
     from the capital city weather station with the longest run of historical
     data. Although not all voters live in the capital city, this is likely to be a
     reasonable proxy for the weather affecting most voters on polling day.
     The regression includes indicators for state/territory effects and year
     effects. The rainfall specification is significant using an indicator for
     rain on election day only, while the temperature regression is significant
     when including the temperature for polling day and the two prior days,
     and then summing the coefficients.

11   Brad T. Gomez, Thomas G. Hansford and George A. Krause, 2007,
     'The Republicans should pray for rain: Weather, turnout, and voting
     in US presidential elections', *Journal of Politics*, 69(3): 649–63.
     Conversely, a US study looked at how rainfall affected protestor
     turnout for the nationwide Tea Party protests on 15 April 2009. In
     places where it rained on protest day ('wet districts'), there were fewer
     protestors than in places where it did not ('dry districts'). This meant
     that the Tea Party movement ended up being stronger in dry districts.
     Consequently, the Republican vote in the November 2010 elections
     was 1 percentage point higher in dry districts than in wet districts.
     See Andreas Madestam, Daniel Shoag, Stan Veuger and David
     Yanagizawa-Drott, 2013, 'Do political protests matter?: Evidence from
     the Tea Party Movement', *Quarterly Journal of Economics*, 128(4):
     1633–85.

12   Andrew Leigh, 2009, 'Does the world economy swing national
     elections?' *Oxford Bulletin of Economics and Statistics*, 71(2): 163–81.

13   Justin Wolfers, 2002, 'Are voters rational? Evidence from Gubernatorial
     elections', Stanford University Graduate School of Business Working
     Paper #1730.

14   Andrew Leigh and Mark McLeish, 2009, 'Are state elections affected
     by the national economy? Evidence from Australia', *Economic Record*,
     85(269): 210–22.

15   This is based on a regression in which the unemployment rate for all
     other states in Australia (except the one under analysis) is instrumented
     with the unemployment rate in the United States. See Table 4, Leigh and
     McLeish, 2009.

16   John Howard interview with Keith Colon and Tony Pilkington on 5AA Adelaide, 22 February 2006.

17   Laura Tingle, 2014, 'Voters vulnerable as luck deserts Coalition', *Australian Financial Review*, 16 December.

18   Alan Kohler, 2013, 'Economics make this election a good one to win', *The Drum*, ABC Online, 3 July.

19   Andrew J. Oswald and Nattavudh Powdthavee, 2010, 'Daughters and left-wing voting', *Review of Economics and Statistics*, 92(2): 213–27. A study using US data has found that men with sisters are more likely to be conservative: Andrew Healy and Neil Malhotra, 2013, 'Childhood socialization and political attitudes: Evidence from a natural experiment', *Journal of Politics*, 75(4): 1–34. Performing a similar analysis on the 1984 Australian data, I find suggestive evidence of a 'sister effect', but the results are not statistically significant.

20   Dalton Conley and Emily Rauscher, 2013, 'The effect of daughters on partisanship and social attitudes toward women', *Sociological Forum*, 28(4): 700–18.

21   Byungkyu Lee and Dalton Conley, 2014, 'Does the gender of offspring affect parental political orientation?', NBER Working Paper No. 20384, NBER: Cambridge, MA.

22   This analysis uses Jonathan Kelley, Clive Bean and M.D.R. Evans, *National Social Science Survey 1987–1988: Inequality*, Australian National University, Canberra. The question is 'Generally speaking, in federal politics do you usually think of yourself as ... Australian Labor Party, Liberal Party, National Party?' The two Coalition parties are combined, and those supporting other parties are dropped from analysis. The partisan difference for men is statistically significant at the 5 per cent level.

23   This example is drawn from Oswald and Powdthave, 2010: 213–27.

24   Peter K. Hatemi, Nathan A. Gillespie, Lindon J. Eaves, Brion S. Maher, Bradley T. Webb, Andrew C. Heath, Sarah E. Medland, David C. Smyth, Harry N. Beeby, Scott D. Gordon, Grant W. Montgomery, Ghu Zhu, Enda M. Byrne and Nicholas G. Martin, 2011, 'A genome-wide analysis of liberal and conservative political attitudes', *Journal of Politics*, 73(1): 271–85. The

researchers use logarithm of odds scores to adjust for the fact that they are carrying out a very large number of simultaneous statistical tests.

25   Jonathan Haidt, 2012, *The Righteous Mind: Why good people are divided by religion and politics*, Pantheon, New York, p. 324.

26   Quoted in Elaine Sciolino, 2004, 'Spain struggles to absorb worst terrorist attack in its history', *The New York Times*, 11 March.

27   Quoted in Sciolino, 2004.

28   Justin Wolfers and Andrew Leigh, 2002, 'Three tools for forecasting federal elections: Lessons from 2001', *Australian Journal of Political Science*, 37(2): 223–40.

29   Scott Eidelman, Christian S. Crandall, Jeffrey A. Goodman and John C. Blanchar, 2012, 'Low-effort thought promotes political conservatism', *Personality and Social Psychology Bulletin*, 38(6): 808–20. The paper also reports corroborating evidence from another experiment which shows that people who have consumed more alcohol are also more likely to express conservative views.

6 Heart Attacks, Close Votes and the Share Market

1   Newspoll reported that in a two-week period, the share of voters dissatisfied with Turnbull's leadership rose from 21% to 58%: Dennis Shanahan, 2009, 'Turnbull smashed by polling', *The Australian*, 29 June, p. 1.

2   Andrew Robb, 2011, *Black Dog Daze: Public life, private demons*, Melbourne University Press, Melbourne, pp. 165–6.

3   This account is from Dennis Shanahan, 2010, 'A fateful decision changed it all for Tony Abbott and the Coalition', *The Australian*, 13 February.

4   In the years 1939 to 2010, the average minimum for 1 December at the Canberra airport weather station was 10.5°C. On 1 December 2009, the minimum temperature was just 6.2°C (author's analysis based on Bureau of Meteorology data).

5   'Hockey congratulates Abbott', 2009, *Sydney Morning Herald*, 1 December.

6   One Liberal parliamentarian (presumably a Hockey supporter) marked the ballot paper 'No' in the Abbott–Turnbull vote. This was classified as an informal vote.

7   'Malcolm Turnbull loses leadership ballot by one vote – and supporter Fran Bailey is away sick', 2009, *Herald Sun*, 2 December.

8   The turnover rate is divided by the number of jurisdictions for which I was able to obtain data (for example, the 1950 estimate includes seven jurisdictions – the six states and the Commonwealth; while the 2010 estimate includes nine jurisdictions – the six states, two territories and the Commonwealth).

9   Cameron Hazlehurst, 2013, *Ten Journeys to Cameron's Farm: An Australian tragedy*, ANU E-Press, Canberra, p. 3.

10   'Mr Menzies leader of UAP', 1939, *The Argus*, 19 April, p. 1.

11   David Day, 2001, *Menzies and Churchill at War: A revealing account of the 1941 struggle for power*, 2nd edn, Simon & Schuster, London.

12   Day's account is disputed by Allan Martin and Patsy Hardy, 1996, *Robert Menzies: A life, Volume 2: 1944–1978*, Melbourne University Press, Melbourne, p. 354; Gerard Henderson, 2008, 'Why Menzies still matters', *Quadrant*, December. See also a discussion of the issue in John Howard, 2014, *The Menzies Era: The years that shaped modern Australia*, HarperCollins, Sydney, pp. 55–6.

13   These stories were brought to my attention by war historian Brad Manera. My accounts draw on excellent biographies of each of the men in the *Australian Dictionary of Biography*.

14   The link between parental death and leadership is originally set out in Lucille Iremonger, 1970, *The Fiery Chariot: A study of British prime ministers and the search for love*, Secker and Warburg, London. I use corrected data on prime ministers from Hugh Berrington, 1974, 'Review Article: The Fiery Chariot: A study of British prime ministers and the search for love', *British Journal of Political Science*, 4(3): 345–69. (Berrington covers twenty-four prime ministers from 1721 to 1940, ending with Neville Chamberlain.) I then updated these data to the present (of the thirteen UK prime ministers to serve since 1940, only one, James Callaghan, lost a parent before age sixteen). For comparison with

the general population, the most appropriate figure seems to be the 1921 British Census. Berrington estimates that 16% of the population lost a parent in childhood (or 13%, if war orphans are excluded). The Phaethon complex is named after a character in Greek mythology who flew too close to the sun, hoping for proof that his father was the sun god.

15   Bob Carr, 2002, *Thoughtlines: Reflections of a Public Man*, Viking, Melbourne, p. 69.

16   David Solomon, 1974, 'Snedden admits ALP win but denies losing', *The Canberra Times*, 30 May, p. 1.

17   After other candidates were eliminated, the initial result was Snedden 29, Bowen 29. Another ballot produced the result Snedden 30, Bowen 29; David Solomon, 1972, 'Snedden faces his first problems', *Canberra Times*, 21 December, p. 3. The result of the March 1975 ballot was Fraser 37, Snedden 27.

18   Bill Hayden, 1996, *Hayden: An autobiography*, Angus & Robertson, Sydney, p. 268.

19   Jenny Hocking, 2008, *Gough Whitlam: A moment in history*, Melbourne University Press, Melbourne, p. 256.

20   The account of Robert Stone's influence on the ballot is drawn from Louise Dodson, 2003, 'How the numbers fell Mark Latham's way', *The Age*, 5 December.

21   McClelland, quoted in Dodson, 2003.

22   Paul J. Burke, 2012, 'Economic growth and political survival', *The B.E. Journal of Macroeconomics*, 12(1) (Contributions), Article 5. The results on within-party changes are from a working paper version, and were omitted from the published version.

23   Costello, quoted in Peter Van Onselen and Wayne Errington, 2008, *John Winston Howard: The definitive biography*, Melbourne University Press, Melbourne, p. 337.

24   van Onselen and Errington, 2008, p. 337.

25   Keating, quoted in Mark Latham, 2005, *The Latham Diaries*, Melbourne University Press, Melbourne, p. 103.

26   Leo Tolstoy, 1865, *War and Peace*, Volume 1.

27   Graham Freudenberg refers to the impact of Wran's throat operation
on his voice: Graham Freudenberg, 2006, 'The voice of Sydney' in Troy
Bramston (ed.), *The Wran Era*, Federation Press, pp. 99–106, 103. See
also 'Wran ordered to rest for month', 1980, *Sydney Morning Herald*,
3 July, p. 1. Bob Ellis summarises the operation as follows: 'The great
loss was the day mistaken doctors cut Neville Wran's throat. That was
Australia's great lost leader, the man with all the qualities to work it out.
There was a moment when he might have come to us, and the moment
was lost, and then his voice was lost, the one thing he couldn't as a
nation's leader afford to lose and that was that. The corner was turned.
And Bob moved into the gap.' (Bob Ellis, 1997, *Goodbye Jerusalem*, 2nd
edn, Random House, Sydney, p. 25.) In a 1986 interview, Wran said,
'I really do [wish I'd gone to Canberra] because I think any politician
worth his salt wants to be on a larger stage.' (Mike Steketee and Milton
Cockburn, 1986, *Wran: An unauthorised biography*, Allen & Unwin,
Sydney, p. 261.) Kim Beazley suggested to me that the operation
performed on Wran was soon to be superseded by medical technology,
and would not have damaged his voice if it had been conducted a few
years later (author's interview with Kim Beazley, 18 March 2014).

28   Benjamin F. Jones and Benjamin A. Olken, 2005, 'Do leaders matter?
National leadership and growth since World War II', *Quarterly Journal
of Economics*, 120(3): 835–64.

29   Benjamin F. Jones and Benjamin A. Olken, 2009, 'Hit or miss? The
effect of assassinations on institutions and war', *American Economic
Journal: Macroeconomics*, 1(2): 55–87.

30   The dates of the 'near miss' assassination attempts listed in Table 7
are: Lon Nol (17 March 1973 and 19 November 1973), Pinochet (7
September 1986), Mao Zedong (September 1961), Hitler (8 November
1939 and 20 July 1944), Sukarno (30 November 1957 and 8 January
1962), Saddam Hussein (8 July 1982), Mussolini (April 1923, 3
September 1924, 7 April 1926, 11 September 1926), and Idi Amin (7
January 1975 and 10 June 1976).

31   Table 8 lists the date upon which it became known that the prime
minister would change (although in most cases, the formal transition

took place). Daily stock market closing prices bracket the news event. Since the 1991 and 2013 changes happened in the evening (after the close of the stock market) the change is from that day's close to the next day's close. For other events, the change is from the previous day's close to that day's close. For election results, the change is from the Friday close to the Monday close (the same is true of Holt's drowning, which occurred on a Sunday). 1945 prices are for the *Argus* Industrials index, covering prices of 25 large companies on Australian stock exchanges. 1949 prices are from the *Sydney Morning Herald*'s Industrials index. 1966–1983 prices are from the Sydney Stock Exchange All Ordinaries index. Subsequent prices are from the Australian Securities Exchange's All Ordinaries Index. In some cases, the ongoing successor was not clear by the next day's close of trading. In 1966 Holt won the party room vote on the same day as Menzies announced his resignation. But in the case of Curtin's death in 1945, it was not unclear whether Deputy Prime Minister Frank Forde would be challenged for the leadership (he ultimately lost a party room vote to Ben Chifley). Similarly, in the case of Holt's death in 1967, it was known immediately that Deputy Prime Minister John McEwen would step in, but it was not known whether the long-term successor would be William McMahon, Paul Hasluck, John Gorton or Allen Fairhall.

32   This analysis is based on share market data across a 7463-day period, from 3 August 1984 to 31 January 2014.

33   One reassuring implication of this result is that politically connected firms do not dominate the Australian sharemarket. By contrast, see the studies cited in Eric Zitzewitz, 2012, 'Forensic economics', *Journal of Economic Literature*, 50(3): 731–69.

34   Fred Daly, 1977, *From Curtin to Kerr*, Sun Books, Melbourne, p. 196.

35   Analysing members of the forty-fourth parliament (and controlling for tenure) I find that whether someone entered parliament when their side was in opposition or government had no impact on whether they served in cabinet or shadow cabinet.

36   Michael Dalvean, 2012, 'The selection of cabinet ministers in the Australian federal parliament', PhD thesis, School of Politics and International Relations, Australian National University, Canberra, pp. 281–305.

37 Blanche D'Alpuget, 2010, *Hawke: The prime minister*, Melbourne University Press, Melbourne, p. 26.

38 'He inherited me ... He'd had these discussions with staff – I don't know how seriously, by the way, but serious enough for me to say, "Bob, you try and touch me as Shadow Treasurer, and I'll invoke the Harry Truman Doctrine of massive retaliation – and I mean massive."': Paul Keating interview with Kerry O'Brien, 2013, *Keating*, Episode 2, ABC TV, 19 November.

39 Recounted in Paul Davey, 2010, *Ninety Not Out: The Nationals 1920–2010*, UNSW Press, Sydney, pp. 155–8.

40 Manfred Cross, 2000, 'Milliner, Bertie Richard (Bert) (1911–1975)', *Australian Dictionary of Biography*, vol. 15, National Centre of Biography, Australian National University, Canberra.

41 Alan Reid, 1975, 'Australia: Election 1975', *Australian Women's Weekly*, 17 December, pp. S181–S196.

42 The revelation that the position of governor-general was offered to Kenneth Myer and Frank Crean before John Kerr is contained in Geoffrey Bolton, 2014, *Paul Hasluck: A life*, UWA Publishing, Perth, pp. 451–2.

43 Paul Kelly, 1995, *November 1975: The inside story of Australia's greatest political crisis*, Allen & Unwin, Sydney, p. 79.

44 For accounts of the Plácido Domingo speech, see Michael Gordon, 1993, *Paul Keating: A question of leadership*, University of Queensland Press, Brisbane, pp. 1–11; Steve Lewis, 2014, *Stand and Deliver: Fifty years of the National Press Club of Australia*, Black Inc., Melbourne, chapter 13.

45 Paul Keating, Address to the National Press Club of Australia, 7 December 1990.

46 See Michael Gordon, 1993, *Paul Keating: A question of leadership*, University of Queensland Press, Brisbane, p. 21.

47 Nassir Ghaemi, 2012, *A First-Rate Madness: Uncovering the links between leadership and mental illness*, Penguin, New York, p. 37.

48 Ghaemi, 2012, p. 217.

49   Ghaemi, 2012, p. 217.

50   Robert James, 1970, *Churchill: A study in failure, 1900–1939*, Penguin, London, p. 385.

51   See, for example, Paul 't Hart and Matt Laing, 2008, 'Strident strategist: Billy Hughes at war 1915–1919', Lecture for the Prime Ministers Research Centre, Old Parliament House, 3 September 2008, Working Paper, Political Science Program, Research School of Social Sciences, Australian National University.

52   The quote is often attributed to Macmillan, though the exact context is disputed.

7 Climate, Baby Bonus and Recession

1   John Howard, Speech to the Melbourne Press Club, 17 July 2007.

2   John Howard, 'One religion is enough', Global Warming Policy Foundation, London, 5 November 2013.

3   Alex Oliver, 2013, *The Lowy Institute Poll 2013*, Lowy Institute, Sydney, p. 25.

4   Ye Li, Eric J. Johnson and Lisa Zaval, 2011, 'Local warming daily temperature change influences belief in global warming', *Psychological Science*, 22(4): 454–9. See also Alex Oliver, 2013, 'The heat is back on climate change', *Interpreter Blog*, Lowy Institute, 11 November.

5   G. Berkeley, 1988, *Three Dialogues between Hylas and Philonous*, Penguin, New York, NY (original work published 1713).

6   Andrew Macintosh and Richard Denniss, 2013, 'Climate change' in Chris Aulich (ed.), *The Gillard Governments: Australian Commonwealth Sdministration 2010–2013*, Melbourne University Publishing, Melbourne, p. 205.

7   Quoted in Marilyn Berger, 1995, 'Assassination in Israel; Yitzhak Rabin, 73, an Israeli soldier turned prime minister and peacemaker', *The New York Times*, 5 November.

8   Editorial, 2015, 'Netanyahu's irredentist Coalition will not last',
    Financial Times, 8 May.

9   Jeff Zeleny, Michael Berens and Geoff Dougherty, 2001, 'Ballots, rules,
    voter error led to 2000 election muddle, review shows', *Chicago Tribune*,
    12 November.

10 Al Gore, 2004, 'Remarks to the Democratic National Convention', 26 July.

11 John Howard, 2014, *The Menzies Era: The years that shaped modern
    Australia*, HarperCollins, Sydney, p. 324.

12 Calwell's policies are outlined in his election launch speeches (delivered
    on 16 November 1961 and 6 November 1963 respectively). These
    speeches are available at <http://electionspeeches.moadoph.gov.au>.

13 Data are from 'House of Representatives – Two Party Preferred Results
    1949 – Present', available at <www.aec.gov.au/elections/australian_
    electoral_history/house_of_representative_1949_present.htm>.

14 Peter Brent, quoted in Robin Tennant-Wood, 2013, 'Seventeen Days', in
    Aulich (ed.), 2013, p. 22.

15 Gwynneth Singleton, 2013, 'The legislative record of a "hung"
    parliament' in Aulich (ed.), 2013, p. 49.

16 Singleton, 2013, p. 49.

17 Singleton, 2013, pp. 50–1.

18 Latham's announcement came via a media statement on 10 February
    2004. John Howard's followed on 12 February 2004.

19 David Wroe, 2004, 'Latham in "baby bonus" pitch', *The Age*, 1 April
    2004.

20 See George Megalogenis, 2012, *The Australian Moment: How we were
    made for these times*, Penguin, Melbourne, pp. 208–9. As Megalogenis
    points out, Australia did indisputably experience two successive
    quarters of negative growth in the first half of 1991, but by the time
    these figures were announced, Keating was on the backbench, having
    failed in his first leadership challenge.

8 Gaffes, Leaks and Superficiality

1   John Hewson interview with Mike Willesee, 3 March 1993.

2   On Hewson's rejection of one-on-one interviews, see Alan Ramsey, 1993, 'Hot pies, cold pies and pie-eaters', *Sydney Morning Herald*, 6 March, p. 27.

3   The full interview between Jaymes Diaz and John Hill is available at <www.youtube.com/watch?v=TrQPXXHUilU>.

4   Nick Leys, 2013, 'Ten questions: John Hill', *The Australian*, 19 August.

5   Jeremy Paxman interview with Michael Parkinson, *BBC One*, 9 November 2002.

6   Angela Cuming, 'I've been around long enough to know a proposition', *Sydney Morning Herald*, 30 August 2005. Brogden had also been under fire for pinching the bottom of another female journalist, and referring to Helena Carr as a 'mail order bride'.

7   Robert Ray, quoted in Australian Senate, 2010, 'Throwing light into dark corners: Senate estimates and executive accountability', Papers on Parliament No. 54, Canberra.

8   'Peter Reith calls for end to Telecard affair', *ABC AM*, 16 October 2000.

9   The transcript is preserved for posterity at <http://australianpolitics.com/1987/03/23/kennett-peacock-car-phone-conversation.html>. Interestingly, a 1988 intercepted conversation between Graham Richardson and Paul Keating, in which the latter was critical of Prime Minister Bob Hawke, was made available to the *Canberra Times*, who decided not to publish it. See Rodney Tiffen, 1999, *Scandals: Media, politics and corruption in contemporary Australia*, UNSW Press, Sydney, p. 88.

10 Rodney Tiffen, 2005, 'Why Political Plumbers Fail – Hypocrisy and Hyperbole in Leak Control', available at <http://acs-cpanel2.acsinternet.com.au/~rodneyt/wp-content/uploads/2014/02/Why-Political-Plumbers-Fail-Hypocrisy-and-Hyperbole-in-Leak-Control.pdf>.

11 Lindsay Tanner, 2012, *Sideshow: Dumbing down democracy*, Scribe, Melbourne.

12 Email from Annabel Crabb, 17 January 2014.

13 Thomas Eisensee and David Strömberg, 2007, 'News droughts, news floods, and U.S. disaster relief', *Quarterly Journal of Economics*, 122(2): 693–728. For more discussion of this issue, see Andrew Leigh, 2014, *The Economics of Just About Everything*, Allen & Unwin, Sydney, pp. 151–4.

14 Crabb, 2014.

15 Crabb, 2014.

16 The story is told in David Jenkins, 2011, 'Key player in dismantling White Australia policy', *The Age*, 16 May.

17 Michael Wolff, 2010, *The Man Who Owns the News: Inside the secret world of Rupert Murdoch*, Broadway Books, New York, p. 158.

18 Author's interview with Paul Kelly, 9 January 2014.

9 Pundits, Pollsters and Punters

1 My interview on ABC's *The Drum* took place on 11 June 2013, and a transcript is available at <http://andrewleigh.com/4365>. Julia Gillard lost the Labor leadership to Kevin Rudd on 26 June 2013.

2 Phillip Metaxas and Andrew Leigh, 2013, 'The predictive power of political pundits: Prescient or pitiful?' *Media International Australia*, 147: 5–17.

3 Andrew Leigh and Justin Wolfers, 2006, 'Competing approaches to forecasting elections: Economic models, opinion polling and prediction markets' *Economic Record*, 82(258): 325–40.

4 Philip Tetlock, 2005, *Expert Political Judgment: How good is it? How can we know?*, Princeton University Press, Princeton, NJ.

5 Louis Menand, 2005, 'Everybody's an expert', *The New Yorker*, 5 December, pp. 98–101.

6 Nate Silver, 2012, *The Signal and the Noise: Why so many predictions fail – but some don't*, Penguin, New York, NY, loc. 872 (Kindle edition).

For a discussion of the limitations of forecasting house prices, national income, population, employment by industry, the share market, the Australian dollar, and sports games, see Andrew Leigh, 2014, *The Economics of Just About Everything*, Allen & Unwin, Sydney, pp. 157 79.

7   Daniel Kahneman, 2011, *Thinking, Fast and Slow*, Farrar, Straus, Giroux, New York, NY, p. 221.

8   Tetlock, 2005, pp. 20–21.

9   Silver, 2012.

10   Dan Gardner, 2010, *Future Babble: Why expert predictions fail – and why we believe them anyway*, McClelland & Stewart, Toronto, p. 154.

11   Jack Soll and Richard Larrick, 2009, 'Strategies for revising judgment: How (and how well) people use others' opinions', *Journal of Experimental Psychology: Learning, Memory, and Cognition*, 35: 780–805.

12   Jack Treynor, 1987, 'Market efficiency and the bean jar experiment', *Financial Analysts Journal*, 43(3): 50–3. This experiment is outlined in James Surowiecki, 2005, *The Wisdom of Crowds*, Random House, New York, p. 286. Surowiecki only cites the second of Treynor's experiments, while I sum both of them.

13   This example is described in Soll and Larrick, 2009.

14   James Surowiecki, 2005, p. 4.

15   For more details, see http://previousleigh.wordpress.com/2006/06/19/when-one-bad-poll-turns-into-two-front-page-stories/

16   Murray Goot, 'To the second decimal point: How the polls vied to predict the national vote, monitor the marginals and second-guess the senate,' *Julia 2010*, ANU E-Press (2012).

17   Justin Wolfers and Andrew Leigh, 2002, 'Three tools for forecasting federal elections: Lessons from 2001', *Australian Journal of Political Science*, 37(2): 223–40.

18   Andrew Leigh, 2005, 'Economic voting and electoral behavior: How do individual, local and national factors affect the partisan choice?' *Economics and Politics*, 17(2): 265–96.

19   Using the polls' published margin of error (2 to 3 percentage points), suggests that that over the course of the election campaign, the Coalition's probability of winning fluctuated between 1% and 98%. This strains credulity. By contrast, assuming a poll margin of error of 10 percentage points produces a degree of volatility in polls which matches that of the betting market estimates: Leigh and Wolfers, 2006: 325–40. See also Leigh and Wolfers, 2002: 223–40.

20   For an academic analysis, see Simon Jackman, 2005, 'Pooling the polls over an election campaign', *Australian Journal of Political Science*, 40(4): 499–517.

21   David Rothschild and Justin Wolfers, 2013, 'Forecasting elections: Voter intentions versus expectations', Working Paper, Brookings Institution, Washington, DC.

22   Rothschild and Wolfers, 2013, Table 6. This table analyses polls taken within ninety days of the election, which is the largest Australian sample in the paper. Analysing thirty-six Australian polls across three elections, the authors find that 88.9% of expectations polls correctly forecast the winner, compared with 41.7% of intentions polls.

23   Author's transcript of a 1983 video clip, rebroadcast on the ABC *Insiders* program on 4 July 2010 in memory of the late Peter Bowers.

24   See, for example, 'Election bets illegal', *Daily Herald*, 26 May 1913, p. 4; 'North Sydney Odds', *Queensland Times*, 29 November 1922, p. 5; 'Election eve: The betting market', *The Age*, 29 October 1924, p. 9; 'Election betting odds', *Cairns Post*, 2 September 1946, p. 5.

25   For a review, see Justin Wolfers and Eric Zitzewitz, 2004, 'Prediction Markets', *Journal of Economic Perspectives*, 18(2): 107–26.

26   Paul W. Rhode and Koleman S. Strumpf, 2004. 'Historical presidential betting markets', *Journal of Economic Perspectives*, 18(2): 127–42

10   Generosity, Failing Fast and Hyperpartisanship

1   Robert Frank, 2009, 'Success and luck', *Huffington Post*, 2 June.

2   Napoleon Hill, 1937, *Think and Grow Rich*, Ralston Society, pp. 38, 76.

3   Wayne Dyer, 2004, *Staying on the Path*, London, Hay House, p. 16,
     quoted in Esther Eidinow, 2011, *Luck, Fate and Fortune: Antiquity and
     its legacy*, London, I.B. Tauris, p. 16.

4   Mihaly Csikszentmihalyi, 1997, *Finding Flow: The psychology of
     engagement with everyday life*, New York, Basic Books, p. 147, quoted in
     Eidinow, 2011, p. 16.

5   Eidinow, 2011, pp.155–7.

6   The first question asks whether 'Success in life is determined by forces
     outside our control'. The share agreeing is 67% in Germany, 66% in Italy,
     62% in Greece, 43% in Britain and 40% in the United States. The second
     question is 'On a scale of 0 to 10, how important is being lucky to
     getting ahead in life?' The share answering 9 or 10 is 35% in Germany,
     47% in Italy, 38% in Greece, 36% in Spain, 22% in the United States,
     and 21 per cent in Britain: Pew Research Center, 2014, 'Emerging
     and developing economies much more optimistic than rich countries
     about the future', Spring Global Attitudes Survey, Pew, New York, NY,
     Questions 13b and 66g.

7   The survey is the Australian wave of the 2005 *World Values Survey*,
     available online at <www.wvsevsdb.com>. The question (39E) asks, 'In
     the long run, hard work usually brings a better life / Hard work doesn't
     generally bring success – it is more a matter of luck and connections.'
     The scale runs from one to ten, and I split it in the middle. Similar results
     can be found when analysing the question on fate versus control (Q40):
     'Some people believe that individuals can decide their own destiny, while
     others think that it is impossible to escape a predetermined fate. Using
     the following scale where 1 means "everything in life is determined
     by fate" and 10 means that "people shape their fate themselves" please
     indicate which comes closest to your view.'

8   Angela L. Duckworth, Christopher Peterson, Michael D. Matthews and
     Dennis R. Kelly, 2007, 'Grit: Perseverance and passion for long-term
     goals', *Journal of Personality and Social Psychology*, 92(6): 1087–1101.

9   This quote is often mistakenly attributed to others, including
     Thomas Jefferson and Samuel Goldwyn: Garson O'Toole, 2012, 'I'm

a great believer in luck. The harder I work, the more luck I have', Quote Investigator Blog, 21 July 2012, <http://quoteinvestigator. com/2012/07/21/luck-hard-work/>.

10   Branko Milanović, 2008, 'Where in the world are you? Assessing the importance of circumstance and effort in a world of different mean country incomes and (almost) no migration', World Bank, Washington, DC, Policy Research Working Paper 4493.

11   Megan McArdle, 2014, *The Up Side of Down: Bouncing back in business and in life*, Viking Penguin, New York, pp. 202–3.

12   Quoted in Eric Markowitz, 2012, 'Why Silicon Valley loves failures', *Inc Magazine*, 16 August.

13   Markowitz, 2012.

14   Jim Thompson, 1995, *Positive coaching: Building character and self-esteem through sports*, Warde Publishers, Portola Valley, CA. See also David Bornstein, 2011, 'The power of positive coaching', *The New York Times* Opinionator Blog, 20 October.

15   Franklin Roosevelt, fireside chat delivered on 7 May 1933, quoted in Drew Westen, 2007, *The Political Brain: The role of emotion in deciding the fate of the nation*, Public Affairs, New York, p. 39.

16   For example, Franklin Roosevelt is judged the best twentieth-century president in the 2010 Siena poll (238 presidential scholars); the 2009 C-SPAN Survey of residential Leadership (a group of presidential historians); the 2008 *Times* newspaper ranking (eight of its commentators); the 2011 United States Presidency Centre ranking (British specialists in American history); and the 2013 History News Network poll (203 American historians).

17   Robert Menzies, 1967, *Afternoon Light: Some memories of men and events*, Cassell, Melbourne p. 57, quoted in John Howard, 2014, *The Menzies Era: The years that shaped modern Australia*, HarperCollins, Sydney, p. 54.

18   Author's interview with John Howard, 5 December 2014.

19   Brent Schlender and Rick Tetzeli, 2015, *Becoming Steve Jobs: The evolution of a reckless upstart into a visionary leader*, Hachette, London.

20   Burrhus Frederic Skinner, 1948, '"Superstition" in the pigeon', *Journal of Experimental Psychology*, 38(2): 168–72. I am grateful to Thomas McMahon for suggesting this analogy.

21   Jim Chalmers, 2013, *Glory Daze: How a world-beating nation got so down on itself*, Melbourne University Press, Melbourne.

22   Justin Grimmer and Gary King, 2011, 'General purpose computer-assisted clustering and conceptualization', *Proceedings of the National Academy of Sciences*, 108(7): 2643–50.

23   Nolan McCarty, Keith T. Poole and Howard Rosenthal, 2006, *Polarized America: The dance of ideology and unequal riches*, MIT Press, Cambridge, MA. Updated data downloaded from <www.voteview.com>.

24   Jonathan Haidt, 2012, *The Righteous Mind: Why good people are divided by religion and politics*, Pantheon, New York, p. 363. Haidt also finds that a county containing a Whole Foods restaurant has an 89% chance of voting Democratic, while a county containing a Cracker Barrel restaurant has a 62% chance of voting Republican.

25   This analysis uses the Australian Election Study (available for all elections) and the Australian Candidate Study (available for all elections except 1998 and 2013). Unfortunately, comparison is not possible with earlier years, since the ideological question was asked on a scale of 1 to 10 rather than 0 to 10.

26   The authors of the new 'Modest Member' column include Kelly O'Dwyer, Jamie Briggs, Scott Ryan, Dan Tehan and Dean Smith. The analysis is based on a sample of about sixty columns in each era.

27   The question was: 'In presenting the news dealing with political and social issues, do you think that news organizations deal fairly with all sides, or do they tend to favor one side?' From 1985 to 2013, the share of respondents who said that news agencies are 'Politically biased in their reporting' rose from 45% to 63%. Both questions from Pew Research Center, 2013, *Amid Criticism, Support for Media's 'Watchdog' Role Stands Out*, Pew, Washington, DC.

28   For good discussions of this issue, see Paul Starr, 2010, 'Governing in the age of Fox News', *The Atlantic*, January/February; Alan S. Gerber,

Gregory A. Huber, David Doherty and Conor M. Dowling, 'Personality traits and the consumption of political information', *American Politics Research*; Eszter Hargittai, Jason Gallo and Matthew Kane, 2008, 'Cross-ideological discussions among conservative and liberal bloggers', *Public Choice*, 134(1/2).

29 Stefano DellaVigna and Ethan Kaplan, 2007, 'The Fox News effect: Media bias and voting', *Quarterly Journal of Economics*, 122(3): 1187–1234. See also Alan S. Gerber, Dean Karlan and Daniel Bergan, 2009. 'Does the media matter? A field experiment measuring the effect of newspapers on voting behavior and political opinions', *American Economic Journal: Applied Economics*, 1(2): 35–52.

30 Drew Westen, Pavel S. Blagov, Keith Harenski, Clint Kilts and Stephan Hamann, 2006, 'Neural bases of motivated reasoning: An fMRI study of emotional constraints on partisan political judgment in the 2004 US presidential election', *Journal of Cognitive Neuroscience*, 18(11): 1947–58. See also the discussion of the study in Benedict Carey, 2006, 'A shocker: Partisan thought is unconscious', *The New York Times*, 24 January.

31 Geoffrey L.Cohen, 2003, 'Party over policy: The dominating impact of group influence on political beliefs', *Journal of Personality and Social Psychology*, 85(5): 808–22.

32 Solomon Asch, 1951, 'Effects of group pressure on the modification and distortion of judgments', in H. Guetzkow (ed.), *Groups, Leadership and Men*, Carnegie Press, Pittsburgh, PA, pp. 177–90.

33 Charles S. Taber and Milton Lodge, 2006, 'Motivated skepticism in the evaluation of political beliefs', *American Journal of Political Science*, 50(3): 755–69.

34 D.N. Perkins, Michael Farady and Barbara Bushey, 1991, 'Everyday reasoning and the roots of intelligence' in James Voss, David Perkins and Judith Segal (eds), *Informal Reasoning and Education*, Lawrence Erlbaum Associates, Hillsdale, NJ, England, pp. 83–105.

35 Jonathan Haidt, p. 94.

36 Quoted in Ezra Klein, 'Unpopular mandate', *The New Yorker*, 25 June 2012, pp. 30–3.

37   This analysis is based on the 1996–2013 Australian Election Studies, with the sample restricted to those who cast their first preference vote in the House of Representatives for Labor or the Coalition. Surveys before 1996 are not directly comparable (a zero on the 1993 survey is 'very unfavourable', which is a weaker perspective than 'strongly dislike').

38   Jonathan Haidt and Marc Hetherington, 2012, 'Look how far we've come apart', *The New York Times* Campaign Stops Blog, 17 September; Shanto Iyengar, Gaurav Sood and Yphtach Lelkes, 2012, 'Affect, not ideology a social identity perspective on polarization', *Public Opinion Quarterly*, 76(3): 405–31.

39   Both estimates are based on averaging the figures for Democrats and Republicans: Iyengar, Sood and Lelkes, 2012: 405–31.

40   Sixty-three per cent of Americans say that they would be 'fine' about a family member marrying someone of any other race (the survey asked separately about marriage to an African American, a White American, an Hispanic American and an Asian American). By contrast, the same report found that only 27% of religious Americans were fine about a family member marrying an atheist: Pew Research Center, 2010, 'A year after Obama's election: Blacks upbeat about black progress, prospects', Pew, New York, pp. 27–8.

41   Thirty-five per cent of US adults would be upset if their child came out to them: McClatchy-Marist Poll, 2014, 'Views on same-sex marriage: Supporters look to feds, opponents more to states', Marist College Institute for Public Opinion, Poughkeepsie, New York, 15 August.

42   Shanto Iyengar and Sean J. Westwood, 2015, 'Fear and loathing across party lines: New evidence on group polarization', *American Journal of Political Science*, forthcoming.

43   When the cat was described as 'Thatcher's cat', it was approved of by 44% of Conservative partisans, but only 21% of Labour partisans. When described as 'Blair's cat', it was approved of by 27% of Conservative partisans, but 37% of Labour partisans: Robert Ford, 2014, 'Of mousers and men: How politics colours everything we see', in Philip Cowley and Robert Ford (eds), *Sex, Lies and the Ballot Box: 50 things you need to know about British elections*, Biteback Publishing, London.

11 What If?

1   Mark Lawson, 1995, *Idlewild, Or, Everything Is Subject to Change*, Picador, New York. An alternative counterfactual is that Kennedy might have done well, paving the way for Bobby Kennedy (had he not been assassinated) to beat Nixon in 1968: Robert Dallek, 2003, 'JFK Lives', in Robert Cowley (ed.) *What Ifs? of American History: Eminent historians imagine what might have been*, Pan Books, New York, pp. 273–84.

2   For another counterfactual history of the Dismissal, see James Walter, 2006, 'What if Whitlam had won another opportunity to implement his program?' in Stuart Macintyre and Sean Scalmer (eds) *What If? Australian history as it might have been*, Melbourne University Press, Melbourne, pp. 138–62.

3   The canonical database of counterfactual history novels, essays and stories is <www.uchronia.net>, which contains nearly three thousand items.

4   The Martin Luther scenario is at the centre of Kingsley Amis's 1976, *The Alteration*, Jonathan Cape, London.

5   This possibility was raised in Edward Gibbon, *The Decline and Fall of the Roman Empire*, chapter 52.

6   Geoffrey Parker, 1976, 'If the Armada had landed', *History*, 61(203): 358–68.

7   Caleb Carr, 'William Pitt the Elder and the avoidance of the American Revolution' in Cowley (ed.), 2003, pp. 17–42.

8   Barbara W. Tuchman, 1972, 'If Mao had come to Washington: An essay in alternatives', *Foreign Affairs*, 51(1): 44–64.

9   The 1931 essay was reprinted in Winston Churchill, 1961, 'If Lee had not won the Battle of Gettysburg', *The Wisconsin Magazine of History*: 243–51.

10 Jay Winik, 'Beyond the wildest dreams of John Wilkes Booth' in Cowley (ed.), 2003, pp. 127–46.

11 William L. Shirer, 1961, 'If Hitler had won World War II', *Look*, 25: 28–43.

12   Robert O'Connell, 'The Cuban Missile Crisis: Second Holocaust', in Cowley (ed.), 2003, pp. 251–72.

13   Jim Davidson, 'What if Tasmania had become French?' in Macintyre and Scalmer (eds), 2006, *What If? Australian History as it Might Have Been*, Melbourne University Press, Melbourne, pp. 15–28; Marilyn Lake, 'What if Alfred Deakin had made a declaration of Australian independence?', in Macintyre and Scalmer (eds), 2006, pp. 29–44; Peter Read, 'What if Aborigines had never been assimilated?' in Macintyre and Scalmer (eds), 2006, pp. 187–211.

14   Author's interview with Bob Hawke, 7 October 2014.

15   Richard Dawkins, 2000, *Unweaving the Rainbow: Science, delusion and the appetite for wonder*, Houghton Mifflin, Boston, p. 1.

16   Peter Thiel quoted in Ben Horowitz, 2013, *The Hard Thing About Hard Things: Building a business when there are no easy answers*, HarperCollins, New York, 2013, chapter 4. Incidentally, Horowitz argues that for the founder of a technology start-up, it makes sense to ignore statistics and focus only on the deterministic problems.

Acknowledgements

1   Author's interview with Bob Hawke, 7 October 2014.

INDEX